MAKING IT!

REAL STORIES, STRUGGLES & STRATEGIES FOR SUCCESS

Copyright © 2025 by Noelle Randall

All rights reserved. In accordance with the U.S. Copyright Act of 1976, the scanning, uploading, and electronic sharing of any part of the book without the permission of the publisher constitutes unlawful piracy and theft of the author's intellectual property. If you would like to use material from the book (other than for review purposes), prior written permission must be obtained by contacting the publisher at admin@iamsherriewalton.com.

Reviewers may quote brief passages in reviews.

Walton Publishing House

Weston, Florida

www.waltonpublishinghouse.com

Printed in the United States of America

Disclaimer: The advice found within may not be suitable for every individual. This work is purchased with the understanding that neither the author nor the publisher are held responsible for any results. Neither author nor publisher assumes responsibility for errors, omissions, or contrary interpretations of the subject matter herein. Any perceived disparagement of an individual or organization is a misinterpretation.

Library of Congress Cataloging-in-Publication Data under ISBN: 978-1-953993-96-0

Contents

Dedication	IV
Introduction	V
1. BEYOND THE BASICS	3
2. YOUR BEGINNING DOESN'T DICTATE YOUR END	22
3. HOW TO GRADE YOURSELF AND GROW	39
4. OVERCOMING YOUR SITUATION AND BS	61
5. THE HIGH PRICE OF HAVING IT ALL	80
6. PLUG YOUR NOSE AND JUMP	103
7. THE TRANSFORMATION CODE	110
8. A WOMAN TRUCKING	132
9. THE GIFT OF EXPECTATION	149
10. IN THE RING OF LIFE	167
11. READY FOR MORE!	182
MEET THE AUTHORS	186

DEDICATION

To all of my students—past, present, and future: You inspire me every single day.

Just as a parent often learns from their child in ways even their parents never taught them, I have learned more from you than I ever expected—more than from many of my coaches and mentors.

Your stories, your success, and the challenges you've overcome have left a lasting impact on me.

This book is dedicated to each of you.

To your success,

—Noelle

Introduction

"Success is not final; failure is not fatal: It is the courage to continue that counts." – Winston Churchill

Ask ten people what it means to "make it," and you'll get ten different answers. For some, it's building a business from the ground up. For others, it's leaving behind what no longer serves them and starting again with nothing but faith. For many, it's simply surviving another day without giving up. But what all of these definitions have in common is this: to make it is not just to arrive at a destination—it is to endure, evolve, and emerge.

This isn't just another book filled with polished advice or picture-perfect success stories. It's an honest collection of people sharing real experiences, written to meet you right where you are.

Whether you're climbing, crawling, coasting, or crashing, there's a story in these pages that will speak to your season. The authors you're about to meet didn't wait until everything was perfect before they shared their truth. They wrote from the trenches. From the turning points. From the in-between chapters, where most people are too afraid to speak.

This book is a collection of voices from all walks of life—men and women, young and seasoned, business owners, corporate leaders, visionaries, mothers, overcomers, and first-generation dreamers. They come from different backgrounds, cities, struggles, and perspectives. But they have one thing in common: they built something from nothing.

No silver spoons. No shortcuts. No handouts. Just grit, grace, and an unshakable belief that they were meant for more.

You'll read stories about navigating motherhood and entrepreneurship. Faith and fear. Reinvention and recovery. Stories of restoration, resilience, and rising again. Cycles broken. Courage found. Every story is a blueprint of what it looks like to keep going, even when the odds aren't in your favor.

Noelle Randall

BEYOND THE BASICS

Embracing Adaptability in Motherhood and Entrepreneurship

Most people know me as Noelle Randall—the YouTube influencer, real estate mogul, and business coach building my legacy while teaching others to do the same. Many don't know that before the cameras, the real estate deals, and the stages, I was just like so many other women—a wife and a mom, trying to figure out how to create a better future for my family.

People often ask me how I manage to do it all—build multi-million-dollar businesses, appear on YouTube daily, launch real estate crowdfunding opportunities, maintain a profitable real estate portfolio, oversee a nonprofit, and coach and mentor others. The answer isn't some secret formula or superhuman strength. The truth is, my greatest strength comes from being a mom.

Surprisingly, the biggest lessons I've learned in life weren't from my real estate business or self-help books. It has been the everyday life experiences that have shaped my thinking and challenged me to grow.

Life has been my biggest teacher. And what I've come to realize, after years of growth, mistakes, setbacks, and breakthroughs, is this: my real estate business wasn't the most complex challenge I've ever faced —it was motherhood. The journey of motherhood has tested me in ways I've never imagined. However, it has also been the most rewarding challenge of my life. And let me tell you, it's far from easy, no matter how seamless it may look after the lights, stylists, and camera crews do their magic.

Over the years, I've accomplished some pretty amazing things, and I'm proud of the life I've built. Like other women, I am not exempt from the realities of life and the unexpected turns that come with it. I've juggled responsibilities, endured storms, built when I was exhausted, and navigated the unexpected. I used to define my success by the ability to walk away from a corporate VP role and build a business from scratch. I've sustained my business for nearly a decade while raising multiple kids. It wasn't always easy, but I made it happen. But no matter how strong, intelligent, focused, or business-savvy I thought I was, nothing could have prepared me for the journey I'd face with Gavin, my 8-year-old autistic son.

In 2017, my husband and I received the great news that twins were on the way. I was working on my MBA at the time, and let's say, being pregnant while in school wasn't new to us. We were excited, and as parents already, we honestly didn't expect life to be much different. After the twins were born, we devised a plan for each of us to take responsibility for one of the twins. With an already growing family, this would help us lighten the load of adding not one but two babies. It seemed like the perfect plan…until it wasn't.

His twin, our beautiful girl Gabriella, slipped effortlessly into a routine—feeding on schedule, sleeping through the night, and adjusting easily to her new world. Gavin, my sweet boy, had a very different rhythm. He came into this world with his own rules: fussy, unpredictable, and seemingly determined to resist every effort at calm. From the beginning, it was clear we were raising two very different babies.

Getting Gavin to sleep felt like a nightly negotiation. The slightest sound, whether it was the TV turned up too loud or a casual conversation in the next room, would set him off. His cries were loud, urgent, and relentless. Gabriella, on the other hand, was the picture of peace. The noise didn't seem to bother her. She adjusted, adapted, and soothed herself easily. Eventually, things began to settle, or at least, that's what I tried to believe. But deep down, my mother's intuition wouldn't rest. Something felt off. Gavin wasn't hitting the same milestones as his sister. At first, I chalked it up to gender differences. "Boys develop slower," I reminded myself, trying to dismiss the unease. But what I initially brushed off began to take shape as something more serious.

By the time Gavin turned one, the signs were harder to ignore. He had stopped making eye contact. He would cry uncontrollably when left alone, and if I stepped out of the room, even for a moment, his screams pierced the house. These weren't the typical tantrums of toddlerhood. Something deeper was unfolding, and I knew we had to face it.

At two years old, it became even more evident that something was wrong. He still wasn't speaking, and his lack of eye contact was more pronounced. He wasn't interacting with us the way Gabriella did. Then one day, he did something that scared me. He opened the door, ran out of the house, and bolted outside without hesitation. This was a wake-up call for me—it was then that I realized something more serious was happening. I began searching for answers and reading about children with autism. Suddenly, everything clicked. The behaviors I had noticed—the lack of sleep, the need for constant closeness, the difficulty with eye contact—all made sense now. Gavin was autistic. I began to understand that autism wasn't always something you could see on the outside. There were no physical markers, no obvious signs. It was a silent struggle that he was going through.

Although I was convinced he was autistic, receiving the official diagnosis was a different story. I learned that the process would be more than having a pediatrician say, 'I think your child may be autistic.' No, the process was much more complicated. We had to see three specialists to get the diagnosis officially recognized by the insurance company. A pediatric neurologist, a pediatric psychologist, and a pediatrician all had to agree on the diagnosis. Three doctors. Three professional opinions. All of them had to confirm that Gavin was autistic for the diagnosis to be accepted by insurance and deemed permanent.

This process was not quick. It took time, patience, and, honestly, much emotional energy. There were days I felt like I was walking through a maze, trying to piece together all the information, not fully understanding what autism meant for Gavin or me as his mother. I had started this journey confidently. After all, I had already raised three children, worked full-time, and attended school full-time while earning degrees and juggling multiple responsibilities. I thought, "This will be another challenge, but I've been through hard things before. I can handle this too.' 'But as I began to learn more about autism, the complexity of it began to open my eyes in ways I wasn't prepared for.

At the time, I didn't realize that raising Gavin wouldn't just be about getting through or simply managing; it would be about embracing the journey. This wouldn't be like the other challenges I'd overcome. Autism wasn't something you could 'push through.' It required deep understanding, ongoing education, and a willingness to completely rethink how I approached my role as a mother and a businesswoman.

Gavin was definitely on the spectrum, no question about it, and when we finally received the official diagnosis, everything changed. Life as we knew it had shifted, and we were now navigating a new reality. While receiving the diagnosis was a step in the right direction, I was determined to give Gavin as much of a 'normal' life as possible. When the twins turned four, I knew it was time to take the next step and enroll them in school. I felt strongly that school would be an excellent environment for Gavin, but more importantly, I wanted him to have the opportunity to socialize with other children. But at the same time, I knew this would be a giant leap—not just for Gavin, but for me.

Gabby, his twin sister, was also eager to go to school, making it the perfect time for both of them. I enrolled them in a well-regarded daycare and preschool program through Florida's Voluntary Pre-K (VPK) initiative. I was excited, thinking this would be the perfect opportunity for them to grow and learn. However, getting Gavin into his first school experience was nothing like I expected. I tried to prepare myself for the challenges, but no amount of reading or research could have fully prepared me for the reality of what was about to unfold. I signed them both up, purchased their uniforms, and eagerly anticipated their first day of school. But the reality of that day was far from what I had imagined.

From day one, it was chaos! The moment I tried to leave him in his classroom, he screamed and hollered because he didn't want me to leave him. Gavin had an intense attachment to me and was scared of new environments, especially unfamiliar buildings. At that time, Gavin had never been exposed to much outside our home. His fear of leaving home was palpable. We rarely took him to places like the grocery store or public spaces because of his reactions. He was used to the people in the house, which was his comfort zone. So, dropping him off at school was a massive challenge for us both. It was a considerable challenge just getting him to the door, let alone inside the building.

The real struggle began when we finally managed to get Gavin inside the school building. He refused to cooperate with the teacher. He didn't make eye contact, would run off, and often hid in closets. He wouldn't stay in the classroom, and the moment they took him outside for playtime, he became completely fixated on staying there. When it was time to come back inside, he fought them with everything he had. Once on that playground, it was like pulling teeth to get him to leave. He didn't transition well from one activity to the next and it was clear to me then that the road to Gavin's independence and adjustment to school would not be smooth. I had to prepare myself for the long haul, knowing each step forward would be a victory. And this was just the beginning.

At the time, sending Gavin to school with other kids would be good. We hoped he would see their behavior and follow their example. But I quickly learned that autistic children don't operate that way. Gavin wasn't concerned with what the other kids were doing. He didn't care that it was time to come inside or that the other kids were cooperating. He didn't want to follow the rules, and no amount of coaxing would change that.

After a week, the school called me to come pick him up. He had barely lasted a week in the program before they kicked him out. And the worst part? They didn't refund any of the money I had spent on his registration, uniforms, or starter packages. That money was gone. We had no choice but to take him home; honestly, that's where he wanted to be anyway. Gavin was most comfortable at home, in his familiar space.

While learning how to adjust to raising Gavin, my entrepreneurship journey was taking off. I was growing my coaching business and building my real estate portfolio. At the same time, I was learning a great deal about myself as an introverted business owner. Juggling these two worlds was overwhelming. Life wasn't slowing down for me. If anything, it felt like everything was moving at lightning speed, and I was trying to keep up.

I'll be honest—there were moments when I wondered if I was crazy for thinking that I could truly have it all. Could I balance being the mom that Gavin needed while building a multi-million-dollar business? Some days, I doubted myself. The responsibilities were heavy, and sometimes, it felt like the world was moving too fast for me to catch my breath. But despite the doubts, I pressed on. I had no choice—this was my journey, and I was determined to make it work.

This is why I am both passionate and firm when it comes to women in business. If you genuinely want to be successful, you absolutely can. Success isn't reserved for a select few—it's available to anyone willing to put in the work and sacrifice to make it happen. My advice to any woman balancing work and motherhood is simple: go for it. Don't let the idea that you can't have both hold you back. Don't use your kids as an excuse for not achieving your dreams.

I hear so many women complaining about why they can't chase their dreams or accomplish their goals, using their children as a crutch. And while I understand that motherhood is hard, and I'm not here to downplay the struggles we face, I refuse to let anyone think that their children are the reason they can't succeed. The truth is, your children should be the reason you push even harder. They should be the fire that fuels you to be the best version of yourself as a mother and a businesswoman.

We often make the mistake of thinking that to be a good mom, we must put everything aside for our children. But I've learned that being a role model, a woman who shows her children what it means to work hard, chase dreams, and never give up, is the best gift I can give them. Your kids will watch you. They'll see your dedication, your perseverance, and your resilience. And you'll show them they don't need to choose between their family and their dreams—they can have both. It's about being intentional with your time, prioritizing your goals, and asking for help when you need it.

You can achieve your goals.

You can make millions of dollars.

You can build successful businesses.

However, it will require commitment. You must prioritize, get organized, and be intentional with your time. I wake up earlier than everyone else to finish things before my kids are awake. This is how you make it work. I had to make some tough choices, too. I stopped traveling so much. I no longer accept gigs in other cities despite having received requests for events in places like Atlanta, New York, and California. I have to say no. And it's okay to say no. I understood what I wanted to focus on and how to make it work right here. But here's the key: I will never use my kids as an excuse for not chasing my dreams. They are the reason I push harder and make things work.

They are my 'why' and not my crutch.

It's been a long journey, but I've learned a vital lesson. You have to accept your child for who they are, not for what society expects or what other kids are doing. Gavin has taught me that comparing him to others serves no purpose. His path is uniquely his own, and I must let him follow it at his own pace. It's a hard lesson, but it's a crucial one. You have to stop worrying about what other kids are doing and focus on what your child needs. There is no comparison. There is no other path but the one your child is on.

That's where the real growth happens. It occurs when you stop looking outside yourself for validation, stop comparing your journey to someone else's, and stay committed to your path. And you know what? This same lesson applies to business. In entrepreneurship, comparing oneself to others and feeling like one isn't measuring up is a common experience. You see other businesses growing faster and other entrepreneurs getting more recognition, and it can feel like you're falling behind. But here's the truth: just like with Gavin, your business journey is yours and yours alone. There's no one-size-fits-all path to success. No matter how much it seems like everyone else has it figured out, you have to focus on what your business needs and let it grow at its own pace.

When I stopped worrying about what everyone else was doing, that's when I found my true focus. I stopped comparing my success to others and started putting the time and energy into what truly mattered. I became committed to my goals, my dreams, and my path. This is where real breakthroughs happen—when you stop fighting against your path and start working with it.

Your kids should be the reason why you achieve, not the reason why you can't.

One of the moments I hold dearest came when my oldest son, now twenty, was around fifteen or sixteen. He told me how proud he was of me. He had a front-row seat to my evolution—from a corporate professional climbing the traditional ladder to a purpose-driven entrepreneur who walked away from stability to build something of her own. He's witnessed the best-selling books I've authored and brought to life, the steady growth of my YouTube channel, and the impact of my presence on social media. He's been there when strangers approached me in public to say, "Noelle, thank you. Your message changed my life." He saw it all—not from a distance, but up close.

What means the most to me is that through it all, he never saw himself as an interruption or a limitation. He saw his mother pushing forward, chasing her dreams, and achieving them—despite every challenge. And in doing so, he saw what was possible for himself.

That's the message I want to share: your kids should never be an excuse for not pursuing your dreams. They should be why you go after them with everything you've got. I've always ensured my kids knew they were never a burden to me. They are the catalyst for my success. My son knows that. My kids know that. I make sure they understand that no matter how hard things get, nothing comes above them—not my work, not my dreams, nothing. I work hard so they can see that they can achieve whatever they set their minds to.

My kids are not a hindrance, they are my motivation. I make sure my kids know this loud and clear: There are no barriers to success. Nothing is stopping them from achieving their dreams. Like me, they can accomplish anything and should never let anyone, including themselves, limit what they can do.

Allow your kids to become your catalyst. Let them become your motivation. Let them be the reason why you're doing it, not the reason why you can't.

I had to make some tough decisions when I transitioned from working a regular job to being a full-time entrepreneur. My kids were involved in a variety of activities, including basketball, band, robotics, and more. But if I wanted to build my business, I had to put some things on pause. I had to take them out of some activities for a while so I could make time to focus on my goals. I also had to get my kids on a schedule. You need to establish a routine for your kids, and that begins with setting clear boundaries. What time do they go to bed? What time is homework done? For me, my kids went to bed at 8:00 PM every night, and on weekends, it was 9:00 PM. That gave me a few hours at night to catch up on business—returning client calls, sending emails, and working on proposals.

I started my days as early as 4:00 AM or 5:00 AM. Before my kids woke up, I'd do things for myself and my business. That time was crucial for me. It's the time I used to prep, plan, and care for myself. Because you can't pour from an empty cup. Taking that time for yourself is non-negotiable if you're trying to balance entrepreneurship and motherhood.

Let me share something that will save you a ton of stress: stop trying to do everything. You can't be the superhero mom who does all the laundry, cleans the house, cooks every meal, and runs a successful business. I learned that the hard way. I had to learn to delegate. My husband took the kids to school. I have help with the laundry and the cooking. I stopped trying to do everything and just focused on what needed to get done for the business. Don't be afraid to accept help. Let them step in, whether it's your partner, a grandparent, or a trusted friend.

My kids are not a burden to me. They're my motivation. And the truth is, I can't build my business if I'm unwilling to get help and focus on what matters. It's not about doing everything but being present when it matters. I ensure that I'm there fully when I'm with my kids. I greet them in the morning. We talk. I'm not distracted by emails or work when I'm with them. But while they're at school, I work. I make that time count.

As a mom and entrepreneur, you will have to adapt constantly. Raising Gavin has been a journey of adaptation, learning, and growth—not just as a mother but as a person. Being his mother has taught me more about resilience and love than any business deal ever could. When it came to Gavin, I had to make adjustments to my parenting approach.

What worked for my other children doesn't work for him. I had to find something that worked for him, allowing me to focus on my work while being present with him. We had to find our rhythm. As a mom and entrepreneur, you will have to adapt constantly. Accept that your kids might not follow the same path as others. Accept that things won't always go according to plan. But know that you can still achieve your dreams, and you can do it without sacrificing your kids' well-being.

Gavin has only been to school for a few months in total. He spent about six months in school at the age of seven. We tried to enroll him in kindergarten, but it didn't go well. He missed many days, and after attempting to repeat kindergarten, we had to withdraw him from school. He's in therapy and almost ready to return to school this fall. It's been a journey full of challenges, setbacks, and moments where I wondered if we were doing the right thing, but as a mother, I can't help but be proud of his progress.

I would have said no if you had asked me years ago whether I could adapt to raising a child who required so much care and attention. My life was busy—I had a growing business, children to care for, a million things on my plate—and I honestly didn't know how to make room for another layer of responsibility. But now, I know differently. Life has a way of adjusting to what you need. You have to decide to prioritize the things that matter most—your family, your health, and your dreams—and trust that everything else will eventually fall into place.

I look at the journey we've been on with Gavin, and I am so incredibly proud of how far he's come. As challenging as it's been, I wouldn't change a thing. If anything, raising Gavin has made me a better person, a better mother, and even a better businesswoman. It has taught me the value of patience, adaptability, and focusing on what truly matters. Life doesn't always go according to plan, but when you embrace what's in front of you and prioritize what's most important, you'll find a way to make it work.

If you've been telling yourself that a goal is impossible or too big, too far away, or too complicated, stop. My story isn't about perfection but perseverance and progress in facing challenges. You don't need to have everything figured out. You need the will to start, the drive to keep going, and the belief that you can push through the difficult times.

Impossible is just a label, not a fact. What 'impossible' goal have you told yourself you can't achieve? What have you been postponing or putting off because it feels overwhelming?"

Reflect on this for a moment:

- What is one small step you can take toward that goal today?

- What's one obstacle standing in your way—and how can you move past it?

- What fears have you been letting control you, and how can you overcome them?

- What support do you need, and whom can you contact for help or guidance?

- What would it look like if you just permitted yourself to succeed?

Embracing adaptability in motherhood and entrepreneurship isn't just about survival—it's about thriving despite the challenges. Life won't slow down, but you can adjust, prioritize, and continue moving forward. Whether it's navigating the demands of raising a family or scaling your business, adaptability is your greatest asset.

Remember, it's not about figuring it all out—it's about making progress every day, taking those small steps, and adapting as you go. Because no matter where you are, you have the strength to create the life and success you desire. No matter where you are on your journey, you can have it all. You can be a great mom, a fantastic entrepreneur, and anything else you want to be.

The only question is, what are you willing to do to make it happen?

HIT THE MARK

- Adaptability is an entrepreneurial superpower

- Your "why" must be louder than your excuses.

- You don't have to do it all—you have to do what matters.

- There is no one-size-fits-all timeline for success. Growth looks different for everyone.

- Routine creates freedom. The structure enables individuals to lead their homes and companies effectively.

Reflection:

Write this down, and say it out loud:

I have permission to adapt, not stop, when life presents a different course than planned.

Justin Mirche

YOUR BEGINNING DOESN'T DICTATE YOUR END

A Journey of Grit, Growth, and God

I grew up in a trailer on a quiet dirt road in a small town that didn't have much but for a kid like me, it had what I needed. It wasn't glamorous, and we were far from wealthy by most standards. But our home was filled with love, grit, and lessons that would shape my future more than any classroom could. We didn't always have the latest things, but we had each other, and that gave me a foundation stronger than money ever could. Looking back now, those humble beginnings laid the groundwork for something much greater. It's a long way from that trailer to financial freedom, but faith and family have guided every step of the journey, and an unwavering drive to rise—and help others rise, too.

That's why I believe, with everything in me: your beginning doesn't dictate your end. My beginning may not have been surrounded by privilege or overflowing opportunities, but it gave me precisely what I needed, even if I couldn't see it at the time. Looking back, I realized my childhood was quietly shaping me. It taught me grit and perseverance. It gave me a stubborn kind of resilience that refused to quit, even when life didn't give me an easy path forward. I observed my surroundings closely and I decided early on I wanted more than this.

Back then, dreaming big felt like something reserved for other people—something that belonged to families with connections, money, and a roadmap already laid out for them. The idea that I could achieve something meaningful felt almost foreign. My family loved me, no doubt about it. But they struggled to show me that a life beyond mere survival was possible. I didn't inherit wealth. I inherited grit.

As a result, I wanted the opposite of what I had lived. Academics became my refuge. While I couldn't control my environment, I could control my grades. I excelled in the classroom—not because it was easy, but because it gave me a sense of agency in a world that often felt unpredictable. I became a straight-A student. For me, school wasn't just about education; it was my safe space—the one place where effort produced results, where discipline turned into achievement, where I could prove, both to myself and to others, that I was capable of more.

Sports were also part of my life when we could afford them. I ran cross country, wrestled, and played baseball. But there were seasons I had to sit out because we couldn't cover the cost of gear or team dues. I watched other kids take the field while I sat on the sidelines, wishing I could be out there too. Those moments taught me something valuable. I learned to show up, even when it wasn't fair. I learned to excel in school, even when no one expected it from me. I learned to stay committed, even when doors didn't open right away. Those early experiences quietly fueled my resilience. They taught me that although I didn't have the same resources as others, I could still outwork, outlearn, and outlast. In the end, that determination carried me across a finish line no one in my family had ever reached: I became the first—and only—college graduate in my family. That moment felt like crossing into a new world, one no one before me had ever approached.

My father was a blue-collar man, a hard worker through and through. He spent his days as a painter, earning a living through physical work, creating something tangible with his hands every single day. In his world, 'real men' worked with their hands. That was his definition of honest labor, of meaningful work. So, you can imagine, my path felt like a complete contradiction to what he had envisioned for me. I wasn't wired like him. While he saw value in physical work, I was drawn to ideas. I was a bookish, curious kid who loved reading, researching, and spending hours tinkering with puzzles or video games—Atari, Nintendo, you name it.

That was a significant difference between us that often caused friction. My family loved me deeply, but they were more familiar with survival than success. I constantly felt the tension of being misunderstood by my father. He didn't value the things I was good at. He didn't fully understand or support the man I was becoming. Not out of a lack of love, but out of a gap in exposure. He hadn't seen my kind of path before. However, I still carried his work ethic with me. Even if my hands weren't holding a paintbrush, I learned to approach my work with the same determination and pride he modeled every day. I wasn't building with a hammer. I was building in my mind. I loved to think. To solve. To create, not with materials, but with strategies and imagination.

That friction shaped me. It fueled my ambition. I didn't want his life, even though I respected him. But here's something I've come to understand as I've grown: people, even our parents, can't lead us past their own limiting beliefs, their exposure, or their level of personal development. They can't give us what they've never seen, never experienced, or never learned. It wasn't that he didn't love me. It wasn't that he didn't want the best for me. He couldn't guide me into something he hadn't been exposed to himself. And now, looking back, I have nothing but honor and respect for him. He did the best he knew how. He gave me what he could with the tools at his disposal. And for that, I'm forever grateful.

At a young age, I knew I was meant for something different. Something bigger. Sitting smack dab in the middle of lack, even when my world felt small, there was a quiet voice inside me that kept saying, "There's more." I couldn't shake it. That whisper stayed with me, even when circumstances told me otherwise. This voice wouldn't be silent, even amidst poverty and limited exposure. This quiet yet relentless internal voice nudged me to believe in possibilities beyond what was immediately visible. I didn't have mentors or role models showing me the way, but somehow, that still, persistent voice kept nudging me forward, urging me to believe there was a purpose waiting beyond the poverty I'd known.

So, I did what I knew to do to create a better life for myself. I followed the blueprint I'd been handed: Go to college. Get a good job. Work hard. Success will follow. My school counselors encouraged it, and I believed it. I thought earning a degree would be the key that unlocked the doors no one in my family had ever walked through. I enrolled in college and majored in finance, envisioning the life that would follow. I pictured myself suiting up, getting hired by a major firm—Fidelity, Vanguard, maybe even a Wall Street powerhouse—and climbing the ladder to a six-figure dream. I saw myself providing for my family with ease, making my parents proud, and proving that it was possible to break the cycle.

When I graduated, diploma in hand, it felt like I'd finally arrived. Surely, success was next in line—almost as if it were owed to me for all the years of perseverance. The offers came in, but the salaries didn't make sense. The pay was less than a third of what

I was already earning. I had a family to support. A child depends on me. The math didn't make sense. And beyond the paycheck, the roles themselves felt…empty. The corporate world wasn't the fulfillment I had envisioned. Instead, it became a source of quiet disillusionment.

Each day blurred into the next—spreadsheets, meetings, endless tasks that seemed to drain more than they gave. Every morning, I confronted an unsettling question: How could I possibly create a life better than the one I had known? Not knowing how to answer the question, my mind would roam and often my thoughts would end in frustration. Anxiety became my companion, with fears often overshadowing my dreams. It wasn't merely ambition—it was an overwhelming need for my family to thrive rather than survive. I yearned for something beyond the limitations of my past but lacked a clear path. The unknown was intimidating and often debilitating, casting persistent shadows of doubt on my potential.

Each morning, I woke up with a quiet dread. Each evening, I sat with growing frustration. I began to question everything:

Is this really what I worked so hard for?

Is this success?

Did I miss something?

And deeper still: Am I just not cut out for this?

I couldn't shake the feeling that something was missing. I had checked every box and followed every step, yet I still felt stuck in a life that didn't fit.

One pivotal morning, it all came to a head. I woke up profoundly dissatisfied, with a deep knowing that if I didn't make a change, this quiet ache would follow me for the rest of my life. The thought terrified me. But what scared me more was the idea of settling. I was faced with a clear choice: stay imprisoned by fear, or step into the unknown and trust that God had something greater ahead. Despite the very real risk of failure, I chose courage. Staying stagnant was no longer an option.

That realization lit a fire inside me. I remember the exact moment it all clicked. I was driving an hour and a half to a job I hated—sitting in traffic, staring at the road ahead, dreading what waited on the other side. Corporate politics. Lackluster pay. A soul-draining environment where people traded their dreams for a paycheck, year after year. I saw colleagues spend two decades clawing their way to six figures while the company made millions off their efforts. And I thought to myself: That's not going to be my story.

The day I quit was both liberating and terrifying. My wife and I didn't agree at first. She wanted me to stay on the course, keeping a steady paycheck. I understood her concern—we had kids, bills and responsibilities. But something in me couldn't shake the conviction that God was calling me higher. Eventually, we agreed, and I left. It felt like I was taking my first real breath in years.

I landed a role in the software industry as an executive sales rep for a music software company. It wasn't corporate—it was more like organized chaos. But for the first time, I felt alive again. It gave me something invaluable: proof. Proof that you don't need a Fortune 500 job to thrive. Proof that you could carve out your path with passion, purpose, and a willingness to take a risk. When that company eventually sold to a larger corporation, I knew it was my sign. God was nudging me again. It was time to step out and build something of my own.

Of course, I was afraid. I had kids. I had bills. I had doubts. Questions swirled in my mind: Am I chasing a fantasy? Is this discontent a sign that I'm flawed? Should I just be grateful and stay where I am? But over time, I realized something powerful: I wasn't broken. I wasn't crazy. I wasn't ungrateful. I was built for more. And I wasn't wrong for wanting it. What I had mistaken for discontent was my calling. I've learned that when God places unrest in your spirit, it's not to frustrate you—it's to move you.

One day, while helping someone clean up their credit, my wife said something profound but straightforward: "You love this stuff. Why don't you build a business around it?"

That's all it took. The seed was planted. My first business was in the personal credit space. Credit had always fascinated me—how it worked, how it could be leveraged, how it could be rebuilt. I started from scratch. No roadmap. No investors. Just raw belief and a vision. I spent the first year doing pro bono work for mortgage lenders to get my foot in the door.

I wanted to learn everything—how to help people qualify for home loans, how to restructure debt, and how to guide someone from financial frustration to financial freedom. The early days of my entrepreneurial journey tested every ounce of my resolve. I didn't have a blueprint—just determination, grit, and a willingness to figure it out as I went. Diving headfirst into building a business requires an enormous amount of discipline and relentless focus. Every day brought new challenges: learning the ropes of marketing, navigating complex business relationships, and building a network from scratch. Networking, in particular, felt like foreign territory. I wasn't a natural. It was filled with awkward conversations, cold calls that went nowhere, and doors that stayed firmly closed. I didn't let it deter me. I kept showing up and eventually, genuine connections started to form. Slowly, those connections became a source of strength and revenue. That hustle paid off.

Eventually, I secured partnerships with major lending offices—some closing $10 million a year, while others approached $1 billion. However, getting there wasn't easy. I didn't know how to network. I didn't know how to scale. I built every system from the ground up through trial and error. My first small win came when I turned my free work into paying clients. That's when I knew I had something here.

Then came the dips. The economy took a hit. Sales dried up. I had to lay off employees—people I cared about. It was brutal. Humbling. For the first time, the weight of leadership, responsibility, and failure hit me all at once. Looking back, that was the moment my faith became personal. Deep. Real. When the numbers didn't add up, when payroll was due and the account was empty, and when I didn't know how we'd make it through the month, I had no choice but to trust God. Not in theory. Not just in Sunday morning faith. But in a daily, moment-by-moment, "God, You have to show up" kind of faith.

He did.

Fear was always close, whispering doubts, stirring anxiety, threatening to derail me. Fear of failure. Fear of rejection. Fear of financial ruin. But the most painful fear of all was the fear of letting down the people who depended on me. Those fears weren't abstract; they were heavy, real, pressing down on me at every setback. And setbacks came often. Things moved slower than I wanted. Growth proved to be more complicated than I had imagined. I had to scale back on comforts, let go of expectations, and tighten the belt. Some days felt like a step forward, only to be followed by two steps back. It was discouraging.

Yet every small win—every closed deal, every client helped and every debt rekindled my resolve. Every victory, no matter how small, reminded me why I started in the first place.

But the most transformative moment wasn't an external achievement—it was internal. It was faith. My relationship with God became the anchor I didn't know I needed. I began to see every moment—good or bad—as part of His plan.

Every closed door? Protection.

Every delay? Preparation.

Every challenge? A chance to grow.

Faith reshaped everything. Setbacks became setups. Fear turned into wisdom. Uncertainty turned into trust. With God at the center, the impossible started to feel possible. And I realized that true success wasn't just building a business. It was building the man I was called to be.

Today, my original company is still thriving. However, the business I'm most passionate about now is Justin Mirche Consulting. Through this company, we help business owners establish strong financial foundations, develop solid business credit profiles, and secure the necessary funding to grow. We help entrepreneurs structure their systems so they can scale successfully without getting overwhelmed by chaos. This is the company Noelle Randall uses to support her entrepreneurs. Through it, we're able to take people from where they are to where they're called to be—equipped, confident, and capital-ready.

At the center of it all is my faith.

Faith has transformed how I lead, serve, and show up every day. I've learned to stop obsessing over the bottom line. I no longer panic over a bad quarter or lose sleep micromanaging my team. Instead, I lead with grace. I coach with compassion. I trust that if I serve well, the numbers will take care of themselves. When I reflect on those early days—working 90-hour weeks, barely seeing my family, and trying to control every outcome—I realize now that I was leading from a place of fear. Fear of failure. Fear of not being enough. Fear of letting people down.

But today? I lead from faith.

My priorities have shifted: God first, family second, business third. Ironically, when I finally surrendered control, everything fell into place.

As I reflect on this journey, I invite you to reflect on your own. Where are you right now in your personal or professional life? What past experiences are still whispering limiting beliefs into your heart and mind? How has your faith—or the absence of it—shaped the way you see your path?

Gratitude defines my journey now. Beyond financial security, beyond the ability to provide for my family, I've discovered something far greater: purpose. Purpose has given meaning to the struggles, clarity to the setbacks, and joy to the victories. It's no longer just about building wealth—it's about building people, building communities, building a legacy that outlives me. I've come to realize that success isn't measured by what you accumulate but by what you contribute. It's not about how high you climb but how many you lift along the way.

Today, every client I serve, every business owner I equip, every dream I help fund—it all flows from that deeper place of purpose. I wake up knowing that the work I do matters, not just for my family but for the generations that follow. And for that, I'm grateful. Grateful for the journey. Grateful for the lessons. I am grateful to be a kid from a dirt road who now has a seat at the table—not just to eat but to invite others to join. Knowing that my resilience and my faith can help unlock doors for others—that's the real reward. There's nothing more fulfilling than watching someone step boldly into their calling and knowing that you had a hand in helping them get there.

One of the powerful lessons I've learned along the way is this: ignore the external narratives that try to define you. The doubts, the criticisms, the opinions of others? They're just background noise and are irrelevant to your destiny. Over time, my perspective has transformed. I no longer see challenges as threats. I see them as invitations. Invitations to grow. To stretch. To refine the purpose God placed inside me.

Another lesson I've learned is to embrace challenges rather than fear them. I see each obstacle not as a setback, but as an opportunity to grow. Through it all, I've come to understand that success is not measured by the size of your bank account. It's measured by the size of your impact.

Looking ahead, my vision is filled with hope and optimism. This is a transformative era for both dreamers and entrepreneurs. There has never been a better moment to rise, embrace your potential, and boldly pursue the dreams in your heart. No matter what your past looks like, or no matter how difficult or limiting your circumstances have been, your past has no power over your future unless you permit it.

Let my journey stand as living proof of this truth: your beginning does not dictate your end. Move forward and confront your fears courageously. Believe in your ability to overcome and embrace your uncertainty. The extraordinary life you desire? It's not just possible—it's waiting patiently for your decisive action.

The only question is: Will you step forward and seize it?

If I could leave you with one piece of advice, it would be this: Work hard. Grind when you must. But never lose sight of what matters. Because success without peace, without family, without faith- that's not success at all. You can make it. However, you must define what "making it" means to you. And ensure that your definition encompasses joy, freedom, and purpose. A life that looks good to others but feels empty to you is no life at all.

Now that I'm a father, I see things more clearly. I've come to understand that neither my father's way nor my way was completely right—or completely wrong. Both perspectives were necessary. Today, I instill in my children the best of both worlds: the values my father passed down and the lessons I've learned on my journey.

I teach them that academics matter. That knowledge opens doors. But I also teach them that knowledge alone isn't enough. You need grit. You need perseverance. You need a work ethic that refuses to quit, even when life doesn't play fair. And most importantly, I teach them that when you anchor all of it in your education, your work ethic, your perseverance, in faith in God, there's truly nothing you cannot do.

That, to me, is the real legacy: passing on both the wisdom and the faith that built me.

HIT THE MARK

- Don't confuse discomfort with failure. Sometimes, what feels like discontent is divine redirection.

- Your calling may initially appear as confusion.

- You are allowed to want more—even if no one before you ever had it.

- Redefining success is a courageous act.

Reflection

You don't have to come from greatness to become great—you have to answer the call.

Dr. Sherrie Walton

HOW TO GRADE YOURSELF AND GROW

Breaking Cycles That Keep You Stuck

We will all face a pivotal moment in our lives when the life we've built no longer aligns with the version of ourselves we truly want to become. The only way forward is to pivot through honesty, ownership, and the decision to change—even if it costs you your pride, your storyline, or the version of you that others applaud.

I was disillusioned to believe I could handle anything; what doesn't kill you makes you stronger. I lived my life and took pride in that theme. Being assertive meant carrying it all, surviving it all, and still managing to smile through it. I mastered how to wear pain and exhaustion like a badge of honor. It was my proof that I was doing something right.

I was the woman who wore her strength like a crown.

I lived like a walking anthem: "I am woman, hear me roar." Natural childbirth? I did it three times. Built businesses while barely scraping by? Absolutely. Living abroad with school-aged children? Yes—that's also me. I could carry the weight of a thousand things and still smile. I didn't just survive the storm—I hosted conferences wearing bright pink tutu skirts and high heels in the middle of it. Yet, I didn't realize how deeply I had tied my worth to struggle until one day, I looked around and realized I was tired and exhausted. I had built a life I no longer wanted to live.

Life has a way of speaking to us if we take the time to listen. One of my earlier life classes started in 2016. It was a pivotal moment for me. It was the year I started to fearlessly pursue my purpose by entering the speaker circuit and hosting my very first empowerment tour. I was passionate, but I wasn't educated on how to run a business, fund it, or manage my life with a husband and small children. I have always been a risk-taker, often to my detriment. The thing about risk-takers is that we leap without a parachute and wonder why we hit the ground hard. I was out there in this new space, struggling to figure it out with no coach or mentor.

I remember the moment I came face-to-face with my reality and what I saw wasn't pretty. It wasn't broken, exactly, but it was...misaligned. I was doing all the "right" things—showing up, giving back, leading others—but deep down, I had built my identity around a struggle story that no longer served me. The worst part?

I started to glorify it. Because that's what you do when you don't know how to classify it- you create a story about it and blame outer circumstances when things don't turn out as planned.

What happened that day changed my perspective on my life. In the months prior, I had planned an event in another city with limited resources. The event was star-studded, with some of the biggest and wealthiest women. Although financially, things weren't coming together as I had hoped, I prayed for a miracle and headed from Houston to Dallas. That Friday night, my family and I checked into the hotel where I'd be hosting my event the next morning. Everything was prepped. The ballroom was beautiful. Women were flying in. The anticipation felt electric.

As we prepared for the morning of the event, my husband made a quick trip to the car. He returned upstairs with a look I'll never forget.

"The car's gone."

At first, we thought it was stolen. It wasn't...it had been repossessed—right there, in front of the hotel. I had driven into Dallas full of faith and vision, and now, hours before standing on stage, my vehicle had vanished.

And what did I do? I did what I'd always done!

I proceeded as if nothing had happened. I hosted the event, pouring out inspiration and posing for photos. I smiled for magazine bloggers, showed up for radio interviews, and encouraged others. Meanwhile, my reality was unraveling. There was no time to process, no space to pause. I powered through, rented a car the next morning, and headed back to Houston like it was just another chapter in my highlight reel because I had mastered the art of showing up strong—even when I was silently bleeding.

But deep down, I knew this wasn't just a money problem.

This was a me problem, and it was humbling.

That moment connected to the layers of my story that had taken center stage in my life. My story of surviving homelessness, living in a hotel, bootstrapping my business from scratch, and selling myself short over and over again emerged from a mindset that came from an unspoken belief that strength meant silent suffering. To be worthy, I had to earn it the hard way. Now let me be clear—there is pain in the process of becoming. Growth stretches you. Healing breaks you open. But many of us don't know when to stop rehearsing the pain. We replay the story long after the chapter has ended, not realizing we've built our identity around what hurt us. Pain can shape you, but it should never define you.

At some point, I had to ask myself a hard question: *Am I growing through this... or just surviving it?* That's when it hit me—endurance without healing isn't wholeness; it's just prolonged survival. The very traits I used to celebrate—my resilience, my ability to push through, my high threshold for discomfort—weren't signs of growth. They were coping strategies. Armor and adaptations I had learned to wear while navigating pain I never fully processed.

The truth was, I didn't just adapt to dysfunction—I willfully participated in it. I had become it. I didn't just tolerate chaos—I lived in it. But what hit me hardest was the realization that this way of living wasn't even familiar to me. My life started out amazing. I was raised by two parents who loved me deeply. Their story is one of resilience—a family that pulled themselves out of the inner city of Miami, Florida and built a name that would outlast them. They created an environment where excellence was the norm, where faith, hard work, and integrity were just part of who we were. I wasn't pressured—I was supported. They believed in me. They nurtured my gifts. They spoke greatness into me long before I knew what I was capable of. From a young age, I was encouraged to rise, to aim high, and to bring my whole self into every room. And because of that, I learned how to shine.

What I hadn't yet learned was how to pivot when a perfectly planned life suddenly unraveled. When control slipped through my fingers and strategy stopped working, survival introduced itself—not as a bold declaration but as a quiet shift. At first, I thought it was temporary. Just a slight adjustment. Something I could bounce back from with time and effort. So I recalibrated, determined to find my footing. But what I believed was just a short detour turned into years of circling the same broken patterns. Emotionally, financially, mentally—I was struggling, even if no one could see it.

That was the moment I had to get honest with myself. Life wasn't just happening to me. Something inside of me was out of alignment, and whether I realized it or not, I was attracting the same chaos I claimed to resent. Survival had shaped my mindset into one that constantly braced for the next crisis. I had learned to expect disruption and to feel more comfortable in struggle than in stillness. But when I slowed down and remembered who I was at my core—before I learned to make dysfunction feel familiar—I started to return to myself.

I had to sit with some hard questions. When did I start believing that misalignment was a requirement for purpose? When did I trade peace for performance? When did I stop building from the truth and start reacting to trauma? The mirror didn't just show me the version of myself that had been shaped by struggle. It also reminded me of the strength and grounding I still carried. I had roots. I had a foundation. And I remembered who I was before fear, pressure, and survival started calling the shots. Maybe you need that reminder, too. You are not what you've had to adapt to. You are not the pattern. You are the person with the power to change it.

Patterns, Triggers, and Truth

Life is a classroom. We can choose to pass the class the first time it is presented—or we can choose to re-enroll and retake it, over and over, until we get it right. No matter who you are, you can't cheat your way through this class. You can take the accelerated or the at-your-own-pace version, but either way, you won't graduate until you've mastered the lesson. Every level requires a new level of honesty, growth, and responsibility.

One day, after yet another disappointing business failure, I had a sobering realization. I was repeating lessons I should have graduated from. It was time to get honest. No more retaking the same course in survival. It was time to assess what I had learned and what I was avoiding. I had to face the uncomfortable triggers and patterns.

Something had to change—and that something was me. For so long, I pointed outward, blaming the circumstances, the cycles, and the people who didn't show up or follow through. I had given my circumstances too much power over my life. The power to change the outcomes was within me. That moment of raw honesty cracked something open inside me. Accountability was the next class I needed to enroll in, as I was the one contributing to the misalignment in my life. The one sabotaging my success and perpetuating the cycle.

As a coach who helps others find purpose and write their books, I guide people in connecting the dots of their stories. Life has a way of revealing patterns—those repeated lessons and loops that aren't random. They're clues. Purpose clues. Discovery points. When I work with clients, we don't just tell their stories; we craft one that is honest, compelling, and transformative. We take a journey together. We explore who they became in survival mode and uncover who they truly are beneath it. Helping others do that deep work is a calling I don't take lightly. Because there's always a recurring theme running through each of our lives. The real question is: will we choose to notice it and grow, or keep reliving the same chapter again and again?

The Pivot: From Blame to Breakthrough

What if I told you that to reach your definition of success, you're going to have to challenge the way you've always done things? Are you willing to sit down, take an honest inventory, and accept the reality of the life you've created? Would you be willing to stop pointing outward and take full accountability for your role?

Blame is easy. It's familiar. It's safe. It gives us someone or something to hold responsible when life doesn't turn out the way we hoped. And sometimes, the blame feels justified. People have betrayed you. Leaders have misled you. Doors were unfairly slammed shut. That part is real. But here's the part we rarely say out loud: blame doesn't build. It may explain the pain, but it won't produce progress. Blame gives us a narrative, but it doesn't give us momentum. It keeps us rehearsing the same scene long after the curtain should have closed.

If you want to break the cycle and move into something new, you have to stop replaying what they did and start revealing who you are. The real work isn't about fixing everyone else. It's about confronting the parts of you that allow certain things to continue. It's looking in the mirror and asking yourself,

What have I normalized?

What have I tolerated?

What role have I played in staying stuck?

After repeated failures in my business, I had to face something that cut deep. This wasn't just happening to me. It wasn't the clients. It wasn't the economy. It wasn't the systems. It was me—my choices, my mindset, my constant rehearsal of what wasn't working, and the blame I kept placing on everything and everyone except myself.

Then came the wake-up call. That level of honesty is uncomfortable. It's also the gateway to transformation. I had to admit that I was contributing to the very cycles I was desperate to escape. I was stuck in a pattern of conditional healing, waiting for others to change before I gave myself permission to grow. But my breakthrough was never tied to their behavior. It was tied to my decision to stop outsourcing my power. I had to stop handing the pen of my story to the people who hurt me and start writing a new chapter myself.

That is what a pivot really is. Not just a change in direction but a shift in ownership. A sacred decision to stop blaming and start building. When I feel myself slipping back into blame or victim mode, I turn to a simple framework that grounds me: pause, reflect, own, and adjust.

Pause means stopping the spiral, the reaction, the noise. Take a breath. Be still. Growth doesn't begin in movement. It begins in stillness. Reflect by asking the hard questions. What am I avoiding? How did I get here? What part of me keeps recreating this pattern? Own your role without shame. You are not at fault for everything that happened, but you are responsible for what you do next. And then adjust. Make the slight, honest pivot. It doesn't have to be dramatic. Often, the most significant breakthrough happens when you shift your mindset, not your zip code.

This is how we move from blame to breakthrough. Not through perfection but through intentional pivots, one decision at a time.

I share these stories because I believe in transparency. If I am to stand as a teacher in this classroom of life, I must be willing to lay bare my failures, my flaws, and my broken mindsets. I hope that by doing so, it gives you permission to confront your own. Not just to consume wisdom but to apply it.

I have had three failed attempts at business. Not because of bad timing or lack of resources but because I had to face some uncomfortable truths. I had a focus problem. A discipline problem. A don't-tell-me-what-to-do problem. Let's be real. Many of us become entrepreneurs in the name of freedom when sometimes it's just rebellion. We say we want to be in charge, but we aren't always ready for the responsibility that comes with it.

Can I be honest? Before I became an entrepreneur, I was a terrible employee. I would show up right on time, leave early, and use company time for personal tasks without blinking. I didn't see it as dishonest at the time. But I do now. Growth revealed where my habits didn't reflect the best version of me.

Now, when I coach leaders, whether they're writing books or rediscovering their purpose, I help them identify life's patterns not as punishment but as 'purpose clues.' Every life has a recurring theme. Until you confront it, you'll keep reliving it. That's why I created The Purpose Accelerator—to help women like me determine if it's time to pivot or realign. Not every shift requires a complete U-turn. Sometimes, the most minor adjustments lead to the most meaningful breakthroughs.

Here's the truth. We expect growth in children. They get grades, progress reports, and feedback. But who is grading us? Every stage of life is a classroom, and every experience is a test. So let me ask you: Did you learn the lesson? Did you respond, or did you react? Are you growing or just going through the motions?

Let's be honest. Let's assess. Patterns don't just happen. They repeat until you wake up and choose to change. And I'll ask you the same questions I had to ask myself. Are you really okay, or are you just functioning well in your dysfunction? Are you helping everyone else because it's your purpose or because it's your distraction?

You can't counsel your way past a broken pattern. You can't out-serve your need for healing. At some point, you have to stop hiding behind the work and do the work.

You can change. You can do better. You can study. You can retake the test.

That's the beautiful thing about life. It's not a one-time final exam. Every moment is a fresh opportunity to assess where you are and choose differently. Just like in school, if you fail in one area, it doesn't define your whole story. It simply reveals where you need to study deeper, grow wiser, and try again.

And that's the invitation I want to extend to you right now.

Let's pause.

Let's assess.

Take a breath, and ask yourself some fundamental questions:

- Is my life producing the results I truly want?

- Am I aligned with my purpose—or just going through the motions?

- Am I in the relationship I desire—or just enduring one that drains me?

- Am I earning the income I'm capable of—or settling for less than I know I deserve?

- Am I walking in integrity—or hiding behind constant activity?

- Where am I getting A's in life—and where am I silently failing?

Be honest because honesty is the prerequisite for growth.

You can still pass the course.

You can still pivot.

You can still rewrite your story.

All it takes is the courage to grade yourself.

When Purpose Calls, Blame Can't Come

Purpose doesn't always arrive with fireworks or fanfare. More often, it appears in quiet moments and stillness. It appears when you're tired of pretending, when your old excuses stop working, and when the thought of staying in the same cycle feels heavier than the fear of change.

But here's the part we don't talk about enough: purpose will call you out of what's familiar, but it won't let you carry blame with you. Blame does not have clearance. It is too heavy, too bitter, too anchored in the past. You cannot step into what is next with your fists clenched around who did not show up, who did not apologize, or what did not work. Purpose requires open hands.

I had to learn that the hard way. I kept waiting—for the right timing, for other people to change, for life to somehow make the path easier. I believed everything around me needed to align before I could fully become who I was called to be. But purpose does not wait for perfection. It waits for obedience.

Eventually, I had to draw a line in the sand and make a decision. I am not waiting for the apology. I am not waiting for perfect circumstances. I am not waiting for everyone to understand or approve of my journey. I had to move and be willing to move alone if necessary. While blame tried to keep me bitter, purpose was calling me to be better.

I chose better.

That choice was not easy. It cost me comfort. It cost me the storyline where I was always the victim. It even cost me a few relationships. But what I gained was worth it: peace, clarity, alignment, power, and freedom. There is something sacred about the moment you stop rehearsing who hurt you and start making room for who you are becoming. That is when the real pivot happens. That is when you rise. Blame has served its time. But now it's time to release it and step fully into who you were always meant to be.

From Survival to Self-Awareness

There is a kind of exhaustion that sleep does not fix. It is the weight of pretending, of performing, of constantly pushing forward even when you are running on empty. For years, I lived in survival mode, but I did not look like it. I was not curled up in a corner crying.

I was on stage. Running businesses. Coaching others. Smiling in pictures. Quoting scriptures. Living out loud. From the outside, I looked driven, purposeful, and intense. But the truth is, deep down, I was running on fumes.

I had gotten good at surviving. I was so good at it that I mistook it for thriving. I did not realize I was functioning through trauma. I did not see that my constant need to prove, perform, and produce was a mask—one I wore to hide the fear that I was not worthy unless I was doing something exceptional. I had adopted strength as my identity, but it was not real strength. It was self-neglect disguised as hustle.

The hustle, if you're not careful, can fool you. It will give you the high of productivity and disguise it as purpose. But God knows. Life knows. And sooner or later, something will come along to expose the truth. For me, it was failure and disappointment. The kind of repetition that makes you stop and ask, Why does this keep happening? The same situations, dressed in different clothes, kept finding me. Eventually, I had to stop running. I had to face the truth: I was the common denominator in my chaos. That was the moment self-awareness began.

Self-awareness is not always pretty. It is not a candlelit journaling session with soft music playing in the background. It is messy. It is humbling. It is disruptive. It is realizing that your so-called independence is really avoidance and that your 'I got this' attitude is pride. And maybe your busyness is just a way to avoid confronting what you don't want to face.

But here is the gift. Once I became aware, I could begin to heal. I could finally choose something different. Survival had taught me how to get by. But self-awareness taught me how to live.

That is the shift I want for you, too.

Because here is the truth. You cannot heal what you will not admit. You cannot grow from what you keep blaming others for. And you cannot evolve while clinging to the very mindset that has kept you stuck. So, if you have been living on autopilot—just going, just doing, surviving—I challenge you to pause. Take a breath. And ask yourself: Am I really okay? Or have I just learned to function in a state of dysfunction?

I have learned that freedom begins with honesty, and honesty deserves space. This is where I had to pause—and now, I'm inviting you to do the same. Not to prove anything. Not to fix it all at once but to check in with yourself.

Your Report Card: Grade Yourself®

Grading yourself is not easy. Here's what often happens when something touches a nerve or hits too close to home: we shift the focus. We start thinking about other people—the ones who should be reading this, the ones who really need the message. But the truth is, this moment is for you. I'm going to tell you what my childhood pastor used to say from the pulpit every time conviction filled the room: "Don't look at your neighbor—this one is for you."

This isn't a group project. Your grade is what you have earned. Now, before you start pulling out the red pen and giving yourself a permanent F, take a breath. I'm not here to shame you. I'm here to guide you. Just like in school, grades aren't about identity. They're about information. They tell you where you are and where you need to grow.

As my earlier experience shows, change requires more than motivation. It demands honesty. Who I had become was shaped by trauma and survival, not by the true essence of who I am. And the same may be true for you. You are not your mistakes. You are not your past. But it is your responsibility to evaluate the fruit of your life.

So let's assess. Let's be real. Let's be honest. And let's be kind to ourselves in the process.

The Self-Assessment Categories™

(Use an A–F or 1–5 scale—whatever works best for you.)

For each category below, give yourself an honest grade.

1. Mindset

- Do I think positively about myself and my future?
- Do I make decisions from faith or fear?
- Do I believe I'm worthy of success?

2. Discipline & Habits

- Am I consistent with what I say I want to do?
- Do I follow through?
- Is procrastination a pattern?

3. Relationships

- Do life-giving, supportive people surround me?
- Do I set healthy boundaries?
- Am I showing up as the version of myself I want to be?

4. Finances

- Am I managing my money well?

- Where is my money going?

- Am I living above or within my means?

5. Purpose & Calling

- Do I know what I'm called to do in this season?

- Am I aligned with my purpose, or am I just busy?

- Am I building or burying my gifts?

6. Emotional Health

- Am I aware of my triggers and trauma responses?

- Do I process my emotions in healthy ways?

- Do I ask for help when I need it?

7. Spiritual Life

- Am I making time for prayer, reflection, and spiritual growth?

- Am I waiting for peace to begin—or moving in faith as I go?

- Am I making space for stillness or filling every moment to avoid conviction?

Pause + Reflect

Now that you've completed the assessment, take a moment to review your grades in each area. Look at them honestly, without judgment. Then ask yourself:

- Which area am I proud of?

- Which one is hard to admit?

- What am I truly ready to start working on today?

You have taken inventory. Now, remember, this is not about perfection. It is about awareness. Growth begins with honesty, and clarity is power. Wherever you scored yourself low, do not shrink. Lean in. This is not your final score. It is your starting point.

As we close this chapter, I want to leave you with encouragement and a gentle push: You don't need another confirmation or even a sign from heaven. You already have permission to evolve, to shift directions, to break the cycle, and to choose better. You are not too late, too broken, or too far behind. Everything you need to pivot is already inside of you, including wisdom, strength, clarity, and courage. You weren't created to survive merely; you were created to grow, to rise, and to transform. This is your moment. Not to wish. Not to wait. But to walk forward boldly, gracefully, and unapologetically. Your pivot begins now.

HIT THE MARK

- You can't pivot until you're willing to pause. Stillness reveals misalignment.

- Taking ownership is not blame—it's power. It's the decision to stop waiting for someone else to fix what only you can face.

- You're allowed to rewrite your life—even if others are comfortable with your old version.

- Your patterns aren't random—they're revealing. Pay attention to the loops you keep reliving.

Reflection

I've graduated from survival. Now, I'm leading with vision, rooted in clarity, aligned with purpose.

John Raymond

4
OVERCOMING YOUR SITUATION AND BS

Start Making an Impact in Your Life

I was raised in suburban Salt Lake—a small town tucked between the mountains, where everybody knew everybody, and life moved at a steady, predictable pace. The wildest thing was Friday night football or the occasional high school party. I grew up with five sisters. Translation: I learned to be outnumbered, outvoted, and out-talked from an early age. Life was pretty standard on the surface.

For most of my childhood, I believed I would be a professional football player. That was the dream. My idol back then was Jim McMahon. Every time I played football, I imagined I was him, running plays, making passes, and leading my team to victory. I had pictured the path so clearly: high school success, the NFL draft, a Super Bowl ring.

But then high school arrived, and with it, reality. I weighed barely 100 pounds soaking wet, and no matter how much heart I brought to the game, the truth became undeniable. I was not built for the NFL. While the bigger, stronger players were already catching the attention of scouts, I was still trying to fill out my jersey, hoping that effort alone could close the gap between my dream and the reality unfolding before me.

That realization wrecked me. Up until then, football wasn't just something I did—it was who I was. Every practice, every game, and every dream had been tied to that identity.

And the only part of football I didn't love? School.

Early on, I realized that school wasn't designed for the way I learn or the way I think. I hated sitting in a classroom all day, stuck behind a desk, staring at the clock, waiting for the bell to ring. It felt pointless—like we were just being trained to sit still and memorize things we'd never use. I wasn't built for that. I wasn't wired to sit still. I was way more into movement. Sports. Action. Anything physical. I wanted to be out there running, playing, competing. If it involved a ball, a race, or a scoreboard, I was all in. That's where I came alive.

But once football started slipping away, everything else began to unravel as well. Without football, I didn't know who I was—or what I was supposed to be working toward. Somehow, I managed to make it through high school, barely hanging on. I had skipped so many classes that I lost count. Eventually, the principal pulled me aside and said, "You're not going to make it unless you transfer to an alternative school."

So, I did. I packed up my pride and made the switch. I'm not sure if you've ever attended an alternative school, but let's say that's not where the brightest and most promising students are typically sent. You won't find your cum laude there. No honor roll. No college recruiters are walking the halls. It was the place they sent you when the regular system couldn't handle you. It was filled with the kids who couldn't, or wouldn't, fit the mold. It was the last stop before dropping out. Walking through those doors, I felt it. The stares. The rough edges. The unspoken message that nobody here expected much from you, including the teachers. But here's the thing: I didn't have anywhere else to go. I showed up. And somehow, against the odds, I made it through.

That decision changed everything because it was there that I met my wife. It's funny how life works. I thought transferring to that school was the end of the road. It turns out that it was the start of everything that mattered. By nineteen, we were married with kids. While most of my friends were still out chasing parties, changing majors, and figuring out what they wanted to do with their lives, I was figuring out how to be a husband, a father and a provider. I didn't have a blueprint. There wasn't some master plan or mentor walking me through it. I was winging it, learning as I went, hoping I'd get more right than wrong.

What I did know was simple: I had mouths to feed and no time to waste—every decision I made carried weight. Every paycheck mattered. Every day was filled with responsibilities that seemed overwhelming. I did not have the luxury of waiting to figure it out. I had a family depending on me, and failure was not an option.

I accepted the first opportunity that came my way, which was a position with a Fortune 500 company in the restaurant industry. It wasn't glamorous, but it was a paycheck. And once I got in the door, I hustled. I wasn't too proud to wash dishes, wait tables and cover shifts nobody wanted. I learned every position—from the kitchen to the register to the back office. I made it my business to know the place inside and out. I said 'yes' to every challenge and every opportunity, even when I wasn't sure I was ready. Little by little, it paid off.

By the age of 21, I had earned a promotion to store manager, becoming one of the youngest individuals the company had ever appointed to that role. I had the keys and the title. Above all, I held the proof that perseverance and determination could move you forward, even without a prestigious degree or a flawless resume. The journey was not easy, and it was far from perfect. I earned it through effort, resilience, and an unwavering commitment to keep going.

I grew as a leader there, motivating and developing people, watching my team grow, and achieving milestones they never thought possible. The results showed. My store consistently ranked among the top ten out of sixty locations across Utah, and I took great pride in that accomplishment. We were not just hitting numbers; we were building something meaningful.

Despite all of this effort and success, I kept running into the same wall. Every time I applied for a promotion beyond the store level, the response was always, "You're doing great, but we cannot move you up without a college degree." It forced me to face a complex reality. It did not matter that I had proven myself, outperformed managers with more formal credentials, or built one of the strongest teams in the region. The door remained closed. I wasn't just competing against people; I was competing against a system.

At that time, it was a system that valued credentials over lived experience—a system that cared more about the letters after your name than the results you delivered.

Up until then, I believed that if you just worked harder, stayed later, and outperformed everyone else, you'd rise. Merit would speak for itself, and the results would open doors. Life taught me differently. While standing at that ceiling and watching others with less experience but more paper credentials move past me, I realized the ugly truth: the system wasn't designed for hustle alone to win. It was designed to reward those who had learned how to play the game of life.

For a while, that made me angry. However, eventually, the anger gave way to clarity. I could either stay mad at the system or figure out how to beat it. Because if the rules weren't written for me, I would have two choices: play by them or build my own. If I wanted more, I'd have to get it.

The Spark: Personal Development & Shift in Mindset

Around that time, something unexpected happened—I stumbled across a box of old Tony Robbins cassette tapes. I almost tossed them out, but curiosity got the better of me. I popped one into my car stereo, and for the first time in a long time, I felt something spark inside me. It was like hearing a language I didn't even know I needed.

No one had ever discussed goals with me. About vision. About habits and routines. Where I came from, life was about getting by—doing what you had to do, making it through. Nobody was having conversations about growth, mindset, or personal development. That wasn't part of the culture I was familiar with.

This unexpected voice delivered a message I had never heard before. He spoke of possibility and designing a life with intention rather than simply reacting to circumstances. He introduced the idea of choosing who you wanted to become rather than settling for who life had shaped you to be. Until that moment, I had never even considered that such a choice was possible.

Every morning, I placed those tapes into my car stereo on my way to work. Sitting in traffic, I listened as if my life depended on it because, in many ways, it did. I absorbed every word, hungry and desperate for something different, something better. Over time, something inside me began to shift. My mindset started to expand, stretching me beyond the limits of what I had previously believed. The words I heard initially felt foreign, even impossible, yet little by little, I began to believe them. And more importantly, I began to believe in myself.

I realized I did not have to settle for the life I was living. I was not locked into a struggle. I was not doomed to remain stuck. My past did not trap me. It felt as though someone had opened a window in a room where I had not even realized I was suffocating. For the first time, I could see something beyond the walls that had surrounded me. And once you see it, you cannot unsee it. That belief planted a seed, and once that seed took root, nothing in my life looked the same again. I realized I needed a better map.

For the first time, I began to believe there might be a way forward, a way up. That was when the fundamental transformation began. I started writing down my goals. I created visions for my future. I established routines and committed to them. Personal development was no longer just a buzzword; it had become my lifeline.

Not long after, I secured a new job assisting small businesses in obtaining government contracts and developing business plans. It was not glamorous work, but it provided financial stability. More importantly, it introduced me to an entirely new world: entrepreneurs, business owners, and individuals who were boldly creating their paths. As I supported others in building their dreams, I could not shake the persistent feeling that I was still standing on the sidelines. I wanted to be part of that world, not just observing from the edges. I wanted to build wealth, invest, and make an impact.

I faced another roadblock. Every time I tried to level up—whether it was applying for funding, pitching a project, or pursuing bigger opportunities —I kept running into the same two questions: "What's your education?" and "What's your experience?"

I resented those questions. They felt like locked doors without a key. So, at 32 years old, I made a decision: I would go back to school. Balancing full-time work, full-time fatherhood, and full-time studies wasn't going to be easy, but I was committed to it. No excuses.

I enrolled in classes and braced myself for the juggle. But just as I was getting started, life threw a curveball. The recession hit. My consulting job required me to come into the office regularly. "We can't pay you past the next 30 days," they said. I felt the air leave my lungs. Here I was, standing at the starting line of this next chapter, and the rug was already getting pulled out from under me. I had two choices: quit before I even began, or push through. I chose to push.

I took a job at a big box retailer, working 10-hour shifts. I'd get home, check on my wife and kids, and then crack open my textbooks, working on assignments until two or three in the morning. Some nights, I barely slept. But I kept going, day after day, week after week, year after year. I did that grind for four straight years. In the end, I walked across that graduation stage with a finance degree in my hand. As I held that diploma, I realized it wasn't just a piece of paper; it was a symbol of achievement. It was a declaration. Proof that no matter how many doors had been closed in my face, I had found a way to build my own.

The Power of Focus and Identity

Graduation wasn't the finish line; it was the starting gate. Not long after I walked across that stage, I registered my first business. I didn't know everything, but I knew enough to get started. I started picking up side consulting work, helping small business owners navigate contracts, operations, and growth strategies.

However, the more I worked, the more questions I had. I started getting curious about private equity and about acquisitions. How were people buying businesses with little of their own money? How were deals structured? How could I be part of that world? I wanted to learn it all. So, I made another pivotal decision: I returned to school to pursue my MBA in finance. It was another mountain to climb, another demanding season of late nights and early mornings. Throughout it all, I continued to work, take care of my family, and show up fully in every role I held. Along the way, I discovered something powerful: when I commit, I follow through. No exceptions. But I also learned something deeper—how I present myself matters.

When I first began, I would tell people, "I'm trying to get into investing." I had to wait until I hit a particular milestone before I could claim the title. One day, I flipped the script. I stopped saying, 'I'm trying' and started saying, 'I'm an investor.' Like magic, that tiny shift changed everything. Once I fully embraced that identity, everything began to shift. Doors that had once seemed permanently closed started to open. People began to show up. Mentors arrived. Opportunities presented themselves. Deals started to materialize. It felt as if the world had been waiting for me to step confidently into the role I had previously hesitated to claim.

That season of life taught me that what you believe about yourself shapes what others believe about you. You are the author of your narrative. When you walk into a room with the conviction that you belong, people respond accordingly. They mirror your confidence. But you have to see it in yourself first.

During that time, I made a bold move. I quit my job and went into business full-time. I was ready to bet on myself, to take everything I'd learned and build something bigger. That leap became the setup for the biggest test of my life. Out of nowhere, life hit us with the hardest news yet: my wife was diagnosed with cancer.

When I first heard the diagnosis, everything around me blurred. We were both in shock, unable to comprehend how something like this could happen at such a young age. All I could think was, this can't be real. In an instant, every plan, every goal, and every strategy I had worked for seemed irrelevant. Life was no longer about building wealth or closing deals; it was about finding meaning in life. It became about keeping her alive. It became about holding on.

I became her full-time caretaker overnight. Every day revolved around appointments, medications, and side effects. I learned how to read lab reports. How to navigate the medical battles and become her advocate. There were nights I'd lie next to her, watching her sleep, wondering how much more she could take. I wondered if I was strong enough to carry us both. The toll was heavy. On her body. On my spirit. In our marriage.

And quietly, beneath the surface of the routines was the ache of the unknown. The terrifying question no one wanted to say out loud: *What if she doesn't make it?* Every day felt like a delicate balance between hope and fear. Some mornings, she'd wake up strong, joking with the kids, making us believe we could outrun this thing. Other days, she couldn't lift her head off the pillow. It was during that season that I realized just how precious life is and how nothing is promised. We make these plans and often forget that all we have is today.

In the middle of all that fear, that heartbreak, that uncertainty—I kept going. Not because I was fearless.

I kept going **for her.** For the woman who had built a life with me, who had believed in me before I believed in myself.

I kept going **for our family.** For the kids who still needed to see their dad standing tall, even when everything around us felt like it was falling apart.

I kept going for the future I promised her we'd have, because love isn't just what we feel. It's what we do when the weight of the world is pressing down on us. It's the choice to keep building, keep hoping, and keep moving forward—even when every part of you wants to collapse.

Amidst chemo treatments, hospital stays, chaos, and uncertainty, I somehow managed to close two acquisitions. Two businesses. Five million dollars in total revenue. Not because life was easy. I had learned to move forward even when it wasn't perfect. While standing in hospital hallways. At the same time, sitting next to her chemo chair. While praying quietly in the middle of the night.

Can I share something with you? There will never be a "perfect time" to move forward. Life won't pause because you've got big dreams. It won't clear the path just because your intentions are good. Sometimes, the moment you decide to go all in is the exact moment life throws its most brutal punches. That's what happened to me. You have to build even as things are breaking. You have to keep going while you are grieving. You must carry the vision while carrying the weight of everything trying to knock you down. You can continue moving forward, even when life feels like it is falling apart. You can continue building, even amid brokenness. You have to stay focused and remain fully committed.

I was.

Quitting was not an option. It would have been easy to press pause and tell myself, "Not now. It is too much. I will wait until things settle down." However, the reality is that life does not settle down. Challenges do not wait for their turn. Difficult seasons do not reschedule themselves simply because you have goals. If you are not careful, you can spend your entire life waiting for things to "get better" before you take action and move forward. Most individuals overthink their way into inaction. Planning is valuable, but planning alone is not enough. At some point, you must act. You cannot reach second base if you keep one foot on first. Fear will show up every time. That is not a sign of weakness; it is simply your brain's way of trying to protect you.

Growth lives outside your comfort zone. If you never take the step, you will look up six months—or six years—from now and find yourself still sitting on the same idea, asking the same "what if" questions. The people who succeed are the ones who make the phone call. They submit the offer. They write the plan. They take action. They do the thing.

> "The path to success is to take massive, determined action." Tony Robbins

Psychologists have long recognized that action is not merely the result of confidence; it is often the source of it. Research shows that taking even small steps forward triggers a positive feedback loop known as the "progress principle." Each action, no matter how small, reinforces a sense of agency and momentum, gradually building confidence and reducing fear. In other words, we do not wait for motivation to act; we act, and motivation follows. This is why staying in motion is critical. Action disrupts overthinking, shifts focus from fear to progress and builds the internal belief that change is possible.

This is also true for you. The next step you are avoiding is not waiting for you to feel ready—it is waiting for you to move. You do not need the entire plan mapped out. You do not need perfect conditions. You need to begin. Because once you take that first step, you prove to yourself that you are capable.

Taking action is far more mental than it is physical. The real work happens in your mind—overcoming doubt, silencing fear, managing uncertainty, and challenging the narratives that tell you to wait, hesitate, or hold back. Every decision to move forward begins with a mindset shift, not a physical task. Long before you send the email, make the call, or take the next step, you must win the battle in your thoughts. It is your belief, not just your effort, that propels you forward. This is why people with less experience or fewer resources can still outpace those with more—they move because they have trained their minds to move, even when they do not feel entirely ready.

Some of the greatest enemies of action are not external obstacles but internal battles. Fear of failure convinces you that trying and failing is worse than not trying at all, keeping you stuck in place. Perfectionism tells you conditions must be ideal before you begin, leading to endless delays and second-guessing. Imposter syndrome whispers that you are not qualified or worthy, even when you have earned your seat at the table. An overwhelming goal makes it feel so big and unmanageable that avoidance feels like the only option. These mental barriers often seem invisible, but they are powerful forces that can hinder your progress unless you learn to recognize and challenge them.

The way to challenge these enemies of action begins with awareness and intentional practice. Fear of failure loses its grip when you learn to see failure as feedback, a necessary part of growth, rather than a final verdict. Perfectionism is dismantled when you permit yourself to pursue progress instead of flawlessness, recognizing that completing something imperfectly is better than never starting at all. Imposter syndrome can be weakened when you remind yourself of your proven track record and surround yourself with voices that affirm your values and capabilities. And overwhelm becomes manageable when you break significant goals into smaller, actionable steps, focusing only on what you can do next instead of everything that needs to be done. Taking action is not about eliminating fear, doubt, or uncertainty; it is about learning to move forward despite them.

When you are ready to move forward, even when circumstances are not perfect, consider this ACT NOW simple framework to guide you:

A — Acknowledge your fear

Recognize that fear is normal. It does not mean you are unqualified; it is a sign that you are growing. Do not wait for fear to disappear before you take action.

C — Clarify your next step

You don't need a 50-step plan to get started. You need to identify the next step. Break it down into something manageable and actionable. Even small, simple moves are enough to build momentum.

T — Take immediate action

Don't leave this moment without doing something. Go ahead and send the email, make the call, register the LLC, and write the first paragraph. Your action builds confidence.

N — Name your deadline

Ideas without deadlines turn into dreams deferred. Set a clear, non-negotiable timeline for the next steps and stick to it.

O — Own the outcome

Whatever happens, own it. Wins, failures, lessons—they're all part of the process. Stop waiting for permission or perfection. This is your journey.

W — Work on the process

Repeat the process. Keep going. Focus on building consistency. Winners are not the people who achieve perfection; they are the people who continue to show up.

So now ask yourself: What's the next step you've been avoiding? Not the big, perfect, ten-year plan. Just the next step. The phone call. The application. The email. The conversation. Whatever it is, please do it, even if you're scared — especially if you're scared. That fear is proof that you're standing at the edge of growth. The only way out of your situation and excuses is to face them head-on.

ACT NOW! That's where the magic happens. That's where momentum is born. That's where the life you've been waiting for finally starts to unfold.

HIT THE MARK

- You can't build a life waiting for permission.

- It's not a lack of opportunity—it's often a lack of execution. The action builds confidence and dismantles excuses.

- Who you become is shaped more by your decisions than your circumstances.

- Your past doesn't disqualify you. It equips you to help someone else rise.

Reflection

I'm not waiting for perfect conditions—I'm building in the now.

Tunita Bailey

THE HIGH PRICE OF HAVING IT ALL

Women Balancing Marriage, Motherhood & Millions

For years, I chased success. I built businesses, closed deals, and made the kind of money I once only dreamed of. I worked tirelessly to prove myself, break barriers, and secure financial freedom—not just for me but for my family and future generations. And I succeeded...but there was a high cost.

I used to believe that I could have it all—a thriving business, a beautiful family, and a love that could withstand anything. I thought that success would come easily if I worked hard enough, planned well, and stayed true to my vision. But what I didn't realize was that success would demand more from me than I ever imagined.

When I first started in real estate, finance, and construction, I believed success would bring freedom. I wanted to build my empire and finally enjoy the rewards of my hard work. But the reality was different. Success meant late nights, early mornings, and sacrifices I hadn't anticipated. It meant feeling pulled in different directions—my business, my family, my relationships.

The world teaches us that wealth is synonymous with money. The size of our bank accounts often reflects the properties we own and the businesses we build. While money certainly matters, it doesn't define a rich life. I've sat in rooms with millionaires and billionaires, each of them with everything they thought they wanted—yet feeling empty because they lacked love, genuine relationships, or a sense of purpose beyond their work. Meanwhile, I've met people with far less money who were infinitely happier, more fulfilled, and at peace.

Today, as I reflect on my journey of success, one of my greatest lessons is that true wealth isn't just about money. Money is only one part of wealth. Money alone doesn't make you wealthy. Success is meaningless if you have no one to share it with. True wealth is about legacy—what you leave behind in terms of both dollars and impact. I spent so much time chasing financial success that I almost lost sight of what real wealth truly is.

It was this realization that caused me to formulate a new meaning of success.

I began to see beyond the glossy exterior of success.

I realized that real wealth wasn't just about acquiring but about giving—giving of yourself, your time, your love, and your wisdom.

It's about making a difference in the lives of those around you, whether they're family, friends, or even strangers.

The richest moments in life are not those marked by material wealth but rather those filled with shared laughter, deep conversations, and genuine connections. At times, even amid all my achievements, I've missed out on some of life's most beautiful moments because I was too focused on the chase. I had traded time for success, missing opportunities to treasure the very things that make life worth living.

The accurate measure of success is not found in how much you've accumulated but in how much you've impacted. The wealth I have today is not just in dollars but in love, relationships, peace of mind, and the legacy I am leaving behind for my children and the generations that will follow. It's about showing up as your authentic self, authentically, without pretending, and without trying to meet others' expectations. It's about learning to balance ambition with humility, striving for more while appreciating where you are.

And with that realization, I redefined what success meant to me. My focus is on building something that would outlive me—a legacy of love, integrity, and service. Success no longer felt like a solitary journey, but a shared mission—one that required balance, sacrifice, and vision.

As I came to understand this new perspective, I found peace in the realization that I didn't need to "have it all" in the way the world defines it. I didn't need to be everything to everyone, nor did I need to chase an ever-elusive version of perfection. True wealth, the one we all should strive for, is rooted in peace, purpose, and the freedom to live life on my terms.

The Price of Having It All

Truthfully, many of us have bought into what we think success is. It is often depicted as the ultimate goal—the thing we sacrifice for, work tirelessly towards and celebrate once we achieve it. We're told that by working hard enough, planning carefully, and pushing through obstacles, we can have it all: the thriving business, the perfect family, a passionate marriage, and a bank account full of commas and zeros.

But no one tells you that having it all comes at a cost. If you are not careful, success can come at the expense of the very things that make life meaningful. As I climbed the ladder, I felt the weight of expectations growing heavier with each step. I became so focused on achieving more and proving myself that I often overlooked the things that truly mattered—my health, my relationships, and my inner peace. The sleepless nights piled up, the missed moments with loved ones became too frequent, and the silent resentments slowly started to seep in. Before I knew it, I had traded the joy of living for the constant pursuit of success.

For high-achieving women, the price is even higher as we break down the barriers of traditional roles for women, and most of the time, balance feels like a myth. We are expected to be everything to everyone—the devoted wife, the nurturing mother, and the powerful CEO. We're told to excel at work, show up at home, and still find time to care for ourselves.

The truth? It's a struggle. It's not possible. It's not realistic.

When I began my entrepreneurial journey, I recall the sleepless nights, missed moments, and unspoken resentments that started to build in my personal life. At times, I felt like I was running on empty—pushing through the exhaustion, pretending to have it all together, while internally, I struggled to keep up. I had become a master at putting on a brave face, smiling through the chaos, and convincing everyone around me that I had it all figured out. But deep down, I knew the truth: success had shifted the dynamics of my relationships and left me feeling more isolated than I ever imagined.

I lost touch with some of the very things that used to bring me peace—quiet moments with my family, time to nurture myself, and the simple joys of life that success once promised to enhance. Instead, it felt like I was always chasing something, and no matter how much I achieved, it was never quite enough. The more I achieved, the more I realized that I was doing it alone. Something had to change. When I allowed others to define my success, I felt isolated-- like I was running in a race with no finish line. I forgot that the journey itself—filled with love, laughter, and connection—was just as important as the destination.

I also struggled with the unspoken expectation that we can't show vulnerability or weakness because "strong women don't need help"—they can do it all. We've been told that having it all means doing it all. But the reality is that the cost of trying to do everything can be far higher than we ever expected. The pressure to be perfect and the expectation of being a superwoman who can balance everything can take a toll on our mental and emotional health. In keeping silent about our struggles, we miss out on the very connections that help keep us grounded—the support, encouragement, and sense of community that we all need. "Having it all" doesn't mean doing everything perfectly. It means making hard choices about where to invest your time, energy, and focus.

The Struggle for Balance

If you're reading this, chances are, you've experienced it yourself: the pressure to succeed, to prove your worth, to build something greater than what you were given. Maybe you've missed bedtime stories because a business deal demanded your attention or argued with your spouse late into the night about time, priorities, and why you're always working. You've probably been in rooms where men are praised for their drive while women are questioned about how they'll manage it all. You've likely wondered whether the sacrifices you're making are worth it and if you're sacrificing too much.

But here's the thing: high-achieving women don't struggle with balance because they're failing—they struggle because the definition of "having of all" should be defined individually, by their terms. We're taught that having it all means we must juggle every ball in the air perfectly, all the while looking polished and poised. We're told to lean in, to strive, to push through, and to excel, but no one tells us how to balance that with the deep need for self-care, personal connections, or simply resting without guilt.

So, if you've ever asked yourself:

- Can I be successful and still have a strong marriage?

- Can I be a great mother and chase my biggest dreams?

- Can I have it all without feeling like I'm failing everywhere?

The answer is yes.

But not in the way you've been told. Success doesn't come from doing it all perfectly or from meeting society's unrealistic expectations. It comes from redefining what "having it all" means for you, from understanding that true success is about the choices you make, the boundaries you set, and the life you want to create, without feeling pressured to meet every external demand.

It's time to stop believing the myth of balance and start defining success on your terms. It's time to recognize that real success isn't about checking off every box; it's about aligning your ambitions with your values. It's about choosing your passions, your family, your health, and your happiness without guilt. It's about embracing the fact that you don't have to be everything to everyone and that, by setting boundaries and making intentional choices, you are, in fact, more powerful than you ever imagined.

You can be successful and fulfilled.

You can lead your business and lead your life.

You can chase your biggest dreams while still being present for the moments that matter most.

It's time to take control of your definition of success—and to remember that the best version of you doesn't have to look like anyone else's version of perfection. It's easy to fall into the trap of measuring your success by someone else's standards, especially when you're surrounded by societal expectations of what success should look like. However, real fulfillment comes from aligning your life with your unique values, desires, and vision.

What does it mean to you to have it all? For some, it may mean scaling a business, building wealth, and making a meaningful impact in their industry. For others, it might mean cultivating deep relationships, making time for self-care, and living a life rich in experiences. The key is to take the time to define your version of "having it all" and to pursue it with passion and purpose. Stop chasing someone else's dream and start chasing your own. Only then will you find peace, fulfillment, and a success that feels truly yours.

When you stop comparing yourself to others and begin to let go of the idea that success means doing it all or pleasing everyone, that's when the absolute freedom and joy of success truly begin. It's time to create the life you want according to your own rules.

The Reality of Power Couples: The Cost of Success

Power couples often seem like the perfect balance—two people building an empire together, supporting each other, and enjoying the fruits of their labor. From the outside, they appear to have it all—love, success, and the power to influence. But the reality is that success changes things. What we often don't see are the internal shifts that happen behind closed doors. Relationships are tested when careers take off, business demands escalate, and money starts flowing in.

It's easy to assume that achieving success together will strengthen a relationship, but often, success acts as a mirror, revealing weaknesses that might have gone unnoticed otherwise. The problem isn't success itself—it's what success changes. As we rise, roles shift. Priorities change. Power dynamics emerge.

In a relationship where both partners are high achievers, the person who earns more may unintentionally gain more control over decisions, leading to feelings of resentment or imbalance in the partner. This shift is not always conscious, but it can create tension between partners who once felt like equals. Love doesn't automatically adjust to these changes. If neither partner actively navigates them, the very thing they worked for—financial freedom, career success, and business growth—can become the thing that tears them apart.

For many couples, the initial excitement of achieving success together can eventually be overshadowed by the complexities that arise when business takes center stage. The pressures of running a business, managing finances, and dealing with outside expectations can create an emotional distance between partners. If the couple doesn't have the right communication strategies and emotional support systems in place, even the strongest bonds can begin to fray.

The problem isn't success itself—it's what success changes.

- **Roles shift.** Perhaps you began as equals, but now one person is the primary breadwinner while the other feels left behind.

- **Priorities change.** What used to be quality time is now replaced by late-night meetings, travel, and endless work stress.

- **Power dynamics emerge.** The person who earns more

might unknowingly hold more control over decisions, which can cause resentment.

How to Combat Resentment & Keep Love Strong:

1. **Acknowledge the Shift** – If the business has changed your relationship, talk about it. Ignoring it will only exacerbate the situation.

2. **Check in Regularly** – Weekly conversations about more than work—how you're both feeling, what's working, and what's not.

3. **Celebrate Each Other's Wins** – If only one person's success is celebrated, the other will feel invisible. Make space for both partners' dreams.

4. **Reevaluate Expectations** – What worked in the past may no longer be practical. Be flexible in redefining household roles, financial responsibilities, and relationship needs.

5. **Support Goes Both Ways** – The business owner needs to make time for the relationship, and the partner needs to understand the sacrifices required for success.

How to Keep Love Strong Amid Business Demands

When business demands so much attention, it's easy for romance and intimacy to take a backseat. The focus shifts to the hustle, the deal-making, the deadlines, and the never-ending to-do lists. However, without intimacy and emotional connection, a relationship risks transforming into nothing more than a logistical partnership. The spark fades, and what was once a vibrant, passionate relationship becomes a transactional one.

To keep the fire alive, it's essential to prioritize your connection, just as much as you prioritize your career and business. Here are some strategies for maintaining a strong relationship while juggling the demands of success:

1. **Prioritize Date Nights—No Business Talk, No Phones.** One of the most effective ways to keep your relationship alive is to carve out intentional time for just the two of you. It doesn't have to be elaborate or expensive, but it must be consistent. During these date nights, leave work at the door: no business talk, no emails, no phone calls—just pure connection. Use the time to reignite the spark, have fun, and remember why you chose each other in the first place.

2. **Schedule "No Work" Time Where Business is Off-Limits.** Creating boundaries around work is crucial.

Dedicate specific times each day or week when business is off-limits—whether it's during meals, in the evenings, or on weekends. This allows you both to recharge, reconnect, and be fully present with each other without the constant pull of work.

3. **Communicate Desire, Not Just Stress.** In a busy, high-pressure environment, it's easy for conversations to revolve around stress, deadlines, problems, and what's not going well. But it's just as essential to communicate desire, affection, and appreciation. Take time to express your feelings for each other and share what excites you about the future. Let your partner know you're thinking about them, not just the next business venture.

4. **Surprise Each Other with Small Gestures of Love and Affection.** Small, thoughtful gestures can go a long way in nurturing intimacy. Whether it's a handwritten note, a surprise gift, or simply taking a moment to express gratitude, these acts of love show your partner they're still a priority, even amidst the busyness of life. The little things matter just as much as the big moments.

5. **Remember That Physical Connection Isn't Just Sex.** Physical intimacy is essential, but it's not just about sex. It's about touch, eye contact, shared laughter, and the non-verbal ways we connect. A hug after a long day, holding hands during a walk, or sharing a quiet moment can

all help to deepen your bond. Physical connection is the glue that holds a relationship together, even when life gets hectic.

The Coexistence of Success & Love

Success doesn't have to be an either/or situation. It's not about choosing between your business and your relationship—success is about learning how to make both work together. It takes intention, awareness, and commitment to ensure that both your professional and personal lives thrive.

True wealth isn't just about financial freedom—it's about building a life and love that can stand the test of time. When success is aligned with love, when both partners can support each other's dreams without losing sight of their relationship, that's when real fulfillment occurs.

We can have it all—but only if we're intentional about what "having it all" looks like. It's not just about the accolades or the profits; it's about creating a life where both success and love coexist in harmony. And when that happens, everything else falls into place.

The Emotional Cost of Success

Success is celebrated. It's admired. It's respected. However, what people often overlook is the weight that comes with it. The higher you climb, the more isolated you may feel. While success brings recognition and admiration, it also comes with a hidden emotional cost that many overlook. No one prepares you for the pressure of always being "the strong one," the person who carries the weight of expectations from others.

When you're a high achiever, there's this constant pressure to be at the top of your game—always. You become the go-to person, the problem solver, the one everyone turns to for answers. But the truth is, being "the strong one" all the time can be exhausting. You're expected to have it all together, even when you're struggling internally. No one warns you about the loneliness that comes with carrying the weight of your success.

I've built my businesses from the ground up, breaking into industries that weren't designed for women. I've closed multi-million-dollar deals, mentored others to do the same, and created a legacy of financial power. But what most people don't see is the emotional cost of carrying it all. The sleepless nights, the anxiety, the self-doubt, and the moments when you feel like you're giving everything but getting little in return.

The emotional toll of success can be taxing, and it often goes unspoken. However, it's essential to recognize this cost and take steps to safeguard your mental and emotional well-being. Success is not just about what you achieve; it's about how you navigate the emotional journey that accompanies it.

The Pressure of Being "The Strong One"

As women, we are expected to be everything to everyone. We are the leaders, the nurturers, the problem-solvers. We hold our businesses together, we hold our families together, and in the process, we often forget to hold ourselves together.

We don't get to fall apart in public.

We don't get to show fear in the boardroom.

We don't get to admit we're overwhelmed because we're supposed to have it all figured out. Being "the strong one" means people assume you don't need help. But the truth? Strong women need support, too. We need spaces where we don't have to perform, where we don't have to be the mentor, the expert, or the leader, and where we can just be human.

The Shifting Dynamics of Relationships as Success Grows

As you climb the ladder of success, it becomes increasingly clear that the dynamics in your relationships will shift—not just in marriage but in your friendships, family, and social circles. Success has a way of revealing truths, exposing who truly supports you and who doesn't.

At first, it can be exhilarating to have people cheer you on, celebrate your wins, and encourage your ambition. But the higher you rise, the more you start to see the cracks in some relationships. Some people will celebrate your wins until you start winning bigger than they ever imagined. Success becomes a mirror for those around you, and sometimes, it forces them to confront their insecurities and fears.

I've lost friendships with women who once cheered me on—until my success made them uncomfortable. I've felt the subtle distance grow with family members who didn't understand my ambition or who were threatened by my drive. There were relationships where I was expected to shrink, to make myself smaller, so that others wouldn't feel overshadowed. I began to realize that some people prefer you to remain at their level, even if it means sacrificing your potential.

And that's a painful realization, especially when it's coming from people you thought would always be by your side. However, what I've learned through these experiences is that not everyone is meant to accompany you to the next level. Some friendships don't survive growth because your mindset has expanded beyond what your old circles can comprehend. Some relationships will fail because not everyone is secure enough to handle a powerful woman who is fully stepping into her potential.

The Importance of Letting Go

But here's the empowering truth: it's okay. Not everyone is meant to be part of your journey, and that's a hard truth to accept. The key is to be willing to let go of relationships that no longer align with your purpose. Holding onto people out of guilt, comfort, or nostalgia will only hold you back. I had to learn that, for my growth, I needed to stop clinging to relationships that were no longer serving me or contributing to my journey.

It's tempting to hold on to the past, to keep people in your life because they've been there since the beginning. But success is about evolving—becoming more of who you were meant to be. Sometimes, that means allowing certain relationships to fade. And that's not a failure; it's an act of self-preservation and alignment with your highest self.

Success Doesn't Have to Be Lonely

You don't have to carry the weight of success alone. You don't have to shrink to make others feel comfortable. And you don't have to sacrifice genuine connection and love for the sake of ambition. The key to sustainable success is building a life where success and sisterhood can coexist.

Having the right people in your corner makes all the difference. True wealth isn't just about money—it's about the people who walk beside you, who support your dreams, and who empower you to keep going when the path feels too hard. Wealth is about creating a legacy, and that legacy isn't just built on the businesses we build but on the relationships we nurture along the way.

Your tribe will be the ones who remind you that you don't have to choose between success and love, between your dreams and your relationships. The journey will be challenging, but when you walk with the right people by your side, it becomes infinitely more rewarding.

So, keep building your empire, keep chasing your dreams, but also keep nurturing the relationships that feed your soul. Because true success isn't just about the destination—it's about who you become, who you walk with, and the legacy you create along the way.

Money Matters, But So Do Love, Family, and Health

Let me be clear—money is necessary.

- It gives you freedom.

- It allows you to create opportunities for yourself and others.

- It secures your future and helps build generational wealth.

But money can't replace **love**.

It can't replace **time**.

It can't buy **peace of mind**.

If you're so focused on making money that you neglect your relationships, your health, or your happiness, then what are you working for?

I've had moments where I was too busy closing a deal to pick up the phone for a loved one. I've missed birthdays, special events, and small moments that I can never get back.

And I've learned that real wealth is knowing when to step away from business and step into life.

Because at the end of the day, money will always be there to be made—but time is something you can never get back.

Now, as I sit and reflect on my journey, I no longer define my wealth solely by numbers.

Yes, I am a millionaire.

Yes, I have built businesses and secured financial freedom.

Yes, I have achieved generational wealth.

But my real wealth?

The family that surrounds me.

The people I have mentored and empowered.

The peace of knowing I lived life on my terms.

That is the true definition of wealth.

For years, I believed that success was solely measured by the financial milestones I reached. I pushed myself, striving for more, thinking that wealth would bring me fulfillment. But what I've come to realize is that the richness of life doesn't come from the size of your bank account—it comes from the depth of your connections, the purpose behind your actions, and the freedom to live authentically.

Yes, financial success is a powerful tool that can provide opportunities and security. But true wealth goes beyond the material. It's about the people you surround yourself with—the ones who support you, challenge you, and walk with you through every high and low. It's about the legacy you create, not just in terms of money but in the lives you touch and the positive impact you have on others.

True wealth isn't just about financial freedom; it's about the freedom to live fully, to be present, and to honor what matters most. It's about striking a balance between your ambitions and the moments that nourish your soul. It's about finding peace and purpose, regardless of where you are on your journey. And that? That is the most incredible wealth of all.

HIT THE MARK

- Wealth is more than money. It's peace, love, health, presence, and purpose.

- The expectation to be the strong one all the time is unsustainable.

- You must define success on your terms.

- Balance isn't real, but intentional alignment is.

Reflection

My success is not measured by status or numbers, but by how present, peaceful, and purposeful I am.

Alinda Rowley-Jensen

PLUG YOUR NOSE AND JUMP

You're Either In or You're Out

The dust had barely settled. I stood there, staring at the fragments of my life scattered on the ground, and it hit me. In 60 days, rent would be due again. No money left. No job to rely on. There is no safety net. The fear that gripped me was unlike anything I had ever felt. This wasn't just fear of the unknown; this was the fear of falling through the cracks of a life I had built, now crumbling around me.

There was nothing more terrifying than facing this with nothing. I was left alone in the home we had shared. My husband had filed for divorce, and we still lived together under the same roof, pretending we could make it work until the papers were signed. I had to face the brutal truth - our life, the one we had built together, was gone. The comforts I knew were slipping away, and I felt like a failure.

You think you can prepare for something like that, but you can't. The shock waves hit hard. I had to walk away from the life we had created, the one I thought would last forever. He was the love of my life, and at the same time, I hated him. The roller coaster of emotions I went through in those early days was exhausting- anger, love, regret, and hope all mashed together in an emotional whirlwind that left me drained and lost.

But despite all that, one thing was clear: I had no choice. To survive, I had to make money. And not just any money, fast money. A job wouldn't cut it; it would take too long. Within 30 days, my new company was operational. It was terrifying. I felt like I was plunging into dark, murky waters, and I had no idea if I would sink or swim. I was scared out of my mind, but staying stuck was not an option.

I Do Not NEED Someone; I Need MYSELF.

Looking back, I had always relied on my husband. He was the one who handled the "big things." Whether it was finances, decisions about the future, or the weighty responsibilities of life, I trusted that he had it covered. I thought that was enough, but I was wrong. It turns out that trusting unquestioningly led me to this moment alone, blindsided by the reality that the "big things" weren't taken care of at all.

This time had to be different. I had no one to rely on but myself. That's when I made the decision that would change everything: I would never again give away my power. I would take responsibility for every aspect of my life, for better or worse. I knew I couldn't afford to fail, not with children depending on me. But if failure came, I wanted to know that it was because of my own decisions and choices, not because I had trusted someone else to handle it.

The truth is, I didn't need someone else to save me. What I needed was to trust in myself. It wasn't an easy realization, but it was liberating. I wasn't just fighting for survival anymore, I was fighting for control over my destiny. I had to be informed, aware and in charge of every decision. Failure wasn't an option, but the thought of succeeding on my terms, in my way, was intoxicating. That was when I took the first real step toward becoming the person I was meant to be. I didn't need someone to do it for me. I just needed to believe that I was enough.

You Are Always Stronger Than You Think

At that moment, I stopped thinking and started doing it. The action became my only focus. I used the last of my credit, the money I had barely left, and invested it in a mentor. Everyone thought I had lost my mind. My sister, my grandma, and most importantly, my husband at the time all told me it was a scam.

"You'll never make it on your own," they said. "You'll never do anything with this."

Their words echoed in my head, but instead of letting them break me, I let them fuel me. I was determined to prove them all wrong. With a plan in hand, I worked nonstop. I set out to accomplish in 30 days what should have taken 90 to 180 days. The deadlines were impossible, and the pressure was unrelenting. Yet, I pushed through. Morning, noon and night, I worked. I moved forward even when I didn't know what I was doing. Those 30 days felt like years. Every moment was filled with fear, doubt, and exhaustion. But I kept going. I worked past the things I didn't know, past the overwhelming obstacles. I didn't stop to analyze the problems; I just kept driving forward, using the last bit of energy I had to push the idea forward.

I look back now at the first deal—the one that saved me—and I am amazed. How did I manage to pull it off despite all the mistakes I made? How did I succeed when I was so inexperienced, so unsure of myself? It wasn't luck. It was something much deeper strength I hadn't realized I had. A strength I had to find when everyone around me doubted I had it.

When you understand that you are stronger than you think, that's when everything starts to change. Directed action creates results, even if it's messy, even if you don't have all the answers. I didn't let fear paralyze me, and I didn't take the time to question my every move. I just kept moving. That's the power of resilience. Ultimately, what saved me wasn't knowledge or experience. It was my unwillingness to give up, my refusal to let fear and doubt dictate my future. I was stronger than I ever imagined. And when you realize that, nothing can stop you.

The life I have now, the success I've built, it didn't come from having it all figured out. It came from diving headfirst into uncertainty and refusing to sink. It came from trusting myself when no one else was there to trust me. It came from the understanding that I was always stronger than I thought.

So, if you find yourself standing in the rubble of your life, with nothing but fear and uncertainty staring back at you, remember this: you are stronger than you think. You don't need to have all the answers, and you don't need someone else to save you. You need to take the first step, and then the next, and then the one after that.

Because in the end, you're either in or you're out. And I chose to be in full, completely, and unapologetically.

HIT THE MARK

- Messy action beats perfect plans. Progress happens when you move, not when you wait for everything to make sense.

- Others may doubt you, but let that fuel you. Don't spend time proving them wrong—prove yourself right.

- It's not about having it all figured out. It's about showing up when the stakes are high and your heart is shaking.

Reflection

I am no longer waiting to be rescued. I am reclaiming my power and choosing to lead my own life.

Divonica Smith

7
THE TRANSFORMATION CODE
Break Free and Reclaim Your Power

Life is full of defining moments that alter the course of our existence, forcing us to reevaluate, redefine, and reshape who we are. Some of these moments happen suddenly. Others develop gradually like a river carving out a canyon over time. Regardless of how they arrive, these moments demand a transformation—not only in action but in mindset. They reveal what we're made of and invite us to respond with intention. What we choose to do in those defining moments determines the course of our lives.

The truth about these moments is that they rarely announce themselves. They often catch us off guard, showing up when we are most vulnerable, most tired, or most uncertain. But even in those moments when everything feels uncertain, there is something powerful within us: the ability to make a choice. We get to choose transformation over trauma. To rise, not because it's easy, but because the next version of our life depends on it.

We often hear people speak about change as if it is something that happens to us. But true transformation is something we choose. It is an internal revolution, a deliberate decision to step away from what no longer serves us and step into the unknown with faith. It is understood that while circumstances may shape us, they do not define us. We are the architects of our destinies.

I vividly remember one of the most defining moments of my life—the moment I knew something had to change. I was about five or six months pregnant, raising my one-year-old, working, and attending school—all while trying to hold it together and survive. I was staying with my father, who was living in my grandmother's house. One day, my grandmother returned from Mississippi to check on the house, and during her visit, she told my father that I had to leave. Just like that. No conversation with me. No empathy for my situation. Just a directive: I couldn't stay.

My father, instead of protecting me, told me, "You can't stay here. Your grandmother said you have to leave." And in that moment, two things hit me hard: First, my father didn't have my back. And second, I could no longer depend on anyone else for my stability, not even family. I was too young to sign a lease at that time, so getting a place of my own wasn't an immediate option. But that day, I made an internal vow to myself. As soon as I'm able to sign a lease, no one will ever be able to put me out again. I promised myself that my children and I would never be in that position again.

That moment lit a fire in me. It wasn't just about finding a place to live—it was about reclaiming my sense of security, dignity, and power. It was about being responsible for my freedom and not waiting for someone to do it for me. That experience also taught me that sometimes the most painful moments are the very ones that birth your independence and ignite your purpose.

Let the Transformation Begin

We often hear people speak about change as if it is something that happens to us. But true transformation is something we choose. It is an internal revolution, a deliberate decision to step away from what no longer serves us and step into the unknown with faith. It is understood that while circumstances may shape us, they do not define us. We are the architects of our destinies.

During the time my world was turned upside down, I knew I needed to earn some income if I was going to move out. I needed money—fast. I was staring down at the reality that having another baby would change everything. I needed a plan, a paycheck, and a path forward. Sitting in a classroom, overwhelmed and uncertain, I quietly prayed for something—anything—to help me step into this next chapter.

That's when Ms. Denise walked in. At the time, she was just a visitor giving a presentation at the school. I had no idea she'd later become my godmother. She began discussing a program that enabled students to acquire job skills, pursue their education, and earn a salary simultaneously. She had my attention. The second she said 'paid,' my ears perked up. I needed income, and this sounded like divine alignment.

I couldn't reach home soon enough to call her and leave an urgent message. The next day, I called again—more determined than ever. I knew in my heart that this was going to be a life-changing opportunity, and I wasn't going to let it pass me by. Eventually, she called me back, and that one returned call changed the trajectory of my life.

I enrolled in the program, and not only did I gain work experience, job training, and interview skills, but I was also getting paid to do it. I learned how to present myself professionally, how to build a future, and how to keep sharpening my education. I became the star participant of the program. And to this day, I credit that opportunity—and that divine moment of persistence—for setting me on a better path. If I hadn't called her, if I hadn't followed up, my life might have taken a very different turn. That moment was a pivot not just for me but for the child I was carrying. It was the moment I chose not to be a statistic, but to become a story of strength.

That moment taught me something powerful: change doesn't wait for permission—it responds to decision. When I shifted from fear to determination, everything around me began to align. That's the reality of transformation—it often starts inside, long before anything looks different on the outside. The world around you begins to shift the moment you decide to shift your internal world.

Have you ever noticed how, when you change your perspective, suddenly, everything around you seems different? That is the power of transformation—it does not just change you; it changes the way you experience the world. Your mindset is the lens through which you view life, and when that lens shifts, new possibilities emerge. Transformation is not a passive experience. It is not a gentle drifting into a new way of being. It is an active, intentional, and sometimes painful process. It requires dismantling old belief systems, confronting the fears that have kept you stagnant, and being willing to walk away from everything familiar. It requires breaking free from limiting narratives—whether they were imposed by society, family, or past experiences—and reclaiming the power to define your own story.

Transformation is about more than just improving your life. It is about elevating your existence. It's about stepping into a version of yourself that you've always had the potential to become but were too afraid to embrace. This process is not for the faint of heart. It requires courage, resilience, and an unwavering commitment to growth.

At the heart of transformation lies one crucial truth: change begins within. You cannot expect the world around you to change if you are unwilling to do the inner work. It starts with the way you think, the way you speak to yourself, and the way you choose to respond to challenges. The journey will not always be easy, but I promise you this: every step you take toward transformation will be worth it.

However, as with any profound journey, obstacles will arise. The biggest challenge in this process is not the external barriers but the internal ones, such as fear, doubt, and distractions, that will attempt to pull you back into your old patterns. They will whisper that it is safer to stay where you are, that you are not strong enough to change. But that is a lie. You are more powerful than you have been led to believe. You are capable of far more than you have ever imagined. And the moment you decide to claim that truth, the world will begin to shift in your favor.

The Battle Against Distraction

Distractions are the silent thieves of progress. They creep in unnoticed, disguised as obligations, entertainment, or even self-doubt, and before you realize it, days, months, or even years have passed, leaving you stuck in the same place. To truly transform, you must recognize and conquer the distractions that seek to derail your growth.

Distractions come in many forms. Some are external, such as social media, television, endless scrolling through meaningless content, or even the opinions of others. These external distractions are often easy to identify yet difficult to resist. They offer an escape, a reprieve from discomfort, but they also keep us from facing the reality of our lives and taking the necessary steps toward change.

However, the most dangerous distractions are the internal ones, such as fear. Self-doubt. Procrastination. Negative self-talk. These are the invisible barriers that whisper that you are not ready, that you are not capable, that you do not deserve the transformation you seek. They make you hesitate when you should act, make you question your worth when you should be confident, and keep you from stepping into the life that is waiting for you.

I have battled these distractions myself. There were times when I allowed the fear of failure to keep me from even trying. I let the voices of others dictate what I should or should not do, as if they held the key to my destiny. I convinced myself that I needed more time, more knowledge, more validation before I could move forward. But all of these were illusions—excuses wrapped in self-doubt, designed to keep me from stepping into my power.

The moment I realized that distraction was just another form of resistance, everything changed. I stopped seeking approval. I stopped waiting for the "perfect" time. I stopped letting temporary discomfort hold me back from achieving long-term success. Instead, I committed to discipline. I made a conscious decision to be intentional with my time, to guard my focus like a priceless treasure, and to silence the inner dialogue that told me I was not enough.

To transform your life, you must master the art of focus. Here are some ways to do it:

- **Identify Your Distractions**: Be honest with yourself. What is stealing your time? Is it social media? Toxic relationships? Negative thoughts? Recognizing your distractions is the first step to eliminating them.

- **Set Clear Goals**: A vague vision leads to vague results. Define what transformation looks like for you and create a clear, actionable plan.

- **Establish Daily Rituals**: Success is built on habits. Develop daily practices that align with your goals, whether it's reading, meditating, exercising, or setting aside time for reflection.

- **Protect Your Energy**: Not everyone will understand your journey, and not everyone deserves access to your mind and time. Be selective about who and what you allow into your space.

- **Embrace Discomfort**: Growth is uncomfortable. The mind naturally seeks the path of least resistance, but transformation demands that you push beyond comfort into the unknown.

The ability to overcome distractions is not solely about willpower—it's about making a conscious choice every day to stay committed to your vision. The distractions will not disappear overnight, but with persistence, they will lose their power over you. And once you learn to master your focus, you will find that your transformation happens faster than you ever imagined.

The Power of a Mindset Shift

Your mindset is the foundation upon which your transformation is built. It dictates how you view the world, how you respond to challenges, and ultimately, how successful you will be in your journey of growth. A shift in mindset is not just about thinking positively; it is about changing the way you approach life itself.

A fixed mindset keeps you trapped. It convinces you that your abilities are static, that your situation is unchangeable, and that success is reserved for the lucky or the privileged. A growth mindset, on the other hand, allows you to see possibilities where others see obstacles. It embraces the idea that failures are lessons, that setbacks are temporary, and that improvement is always within reach.

To shift your mindset, you must first become aware of your thoughts. Pay attention to the way you speak to yourself. Do you talk yourself out of opportunities? Do you assume you will fail before you even begin? These are signs of a limiting mindset. The key to transformation lies in reprogramming these thought patterns.

Replace doubt with determination. Replace fear with curiosity. Replace self-criticism with self-compassion.

One of the most powerful mindset shifts you can make is understanding that you are not a victim of your circumstances—you are the creator of your reality. This does not mean ignoring hardships or pretending life is easy. It means recognizing that, while you may not control everything that happens to you, you always have control over how you respond to it.

Here are a few strategies to help you cultivate a mindset shift:

- Reframe Negative Thoughts: Instead of saying, "I can't do this," ask, "How can I make this possible?"

- Practice Gratitude: Focusing on what you have rather than what you lack can transform your perspective.

- Embrace failure as an Opportunity for Growth: Every setback is a chance to learn. The most successful people in the world have failed more times than they can count—but they never let failure define them.

- Surround Yourself with Positivity: Your environment plays a massive role in shaping your mindset. Choose to surround yourself with people who inspire and uplift you.

- Develop a Success Ritual: Daily habits, such as journaling, visualization, or affirmations, can reinforce a mindset of success.

When you master your mindset, you unlock a level of freedom that most people will never experience. You stop being held back by fear, by the opinions of others, or by past failures. Instead, you step into your power, fully aware that you are capable of creating the life you desire.

The Chains of Shame and Guilt

Shame and guilt are two of the most destructive emotions that hold people captive, preventing them from stepping into their full potential. Unlike external barriers, which can often be overcome with strategy and effort, these emotions work internally, attacking self-worth and eroding confidence.

Shame is the deeply ingrained belief that something is inherently wrong with you. It convinces you that you are unworthy, that your past mistakes define you, and that you are not deserving of happiness or success. Shame thrives in secrecy—it feeds on silence and grows stronger the longer you suppress it.

Guilt, on the other hand, is the lingering weight of past actions or inactions. Unlike shame, which targets identity, guilt focuses on behavior. It whispers that you should have done more, that you should have known better, and that you are responsible for things beyond your control. While guilt can sometimes serve as a moral compass, too much of it can leave you stuck and unable to move forward.

True transformation requires releasing both shame and guilt. This does not mean denying past experiences but rather acknowledging them, learning from them, and choosing to grow beyond them. The first step in this process is self-forgiveness. You are not your past. You are not your mistakes. You are evolving, learning, and becoming the person you are meant to be.

To break free from the chains of shame and guilt, you must rewrite your internal narrative. Speak to yourself with kindness. Recognize that growth comes from reflection, not self-punishment. The moment you accept your past as a stepping stone rather than a weight holding you down, you step fully into your power.

Resilience: The Key to Lasting Transformation

Resilience is the foundation upon which transformation is built. It is the ability to face adversity, setbacks, and failures without being defeated by them. It is the inner strength that allows you to rise after every fall, to push forward despite obstacles, and to continue believing in your potential even when the odds are stacked against you.

Many people think resilience is something you are either born with or without, but that is not true. Resilience is a skill that can be cultivated. It grows through experience, through the challenges that test you, and through the decision to keep going even when it feels easier to give up. Resilience is not about avoiding difficulties; it is about learning how to navigate them. Life will throw unexpected challenges your way—financial struggles, broken relationships, career disappointments and health issues. But within each challenge lies an opportunity for growth. Instead of viewing hardships as barriers, resilient people see them as stepping stones.

Building resilience begins with adopting a solution-oriented mindset—focusing on what you can do rather than dwelling on what went wrong. Strengthen your inner world through habits like mindfulness, exercise, or prayer, and learn to embrace change as a part of growth rather than something to fear. Surround yourself with people who uplift and support you, and cultivate a daily practice of gratitude. Even in hard seasons, gratitude helps you see the good, reframe your perspective, and stay mentally strong.

Resilience is not about never feeling discouraged or afraid; it is about refusing to let those feelings define you. It's about standing up, even when you've been knocked down, and continuing to pursue your goals despite the obstacles in your way. The stronger your resilience, the more unstoppable your transformation will be.

Overcoming Adversity: Finding Strength in Struggle

Adversity is inevitable. No one is exempt from experiencing hardships, setbacks, or unexpected obstacles in life. However, it is not the adversity itself that defines you—it is how you respond to it. Some people allow challenges to break them, while others use those very same challenges to fuel their transformation. The difference lies in perspective, resilience, and a willingness to learn from every trial.

One of the greatest truths about adversity is that it has the potential to be your greatest teacher. Each difficulty you face carries within it an opportunity for growth, self-discovery, and evolution. Every challenge forces you to dig deeper, tap into your inner strength, and uncover aspects of yourself that may have otherwise remained dormant.

Think about a time when you faced a difficult situation—whether it was financial struggles, the loss of a loved one, a failed relationship, or a personal setback. At the time, it may have felt insurmountable. However, looking back now, you can likely see how that experience has shaped you. Perhaps it made you stronger, taught you resilience, or pushed you toward a new path that ultimately led to something better.

To truly overcome adversity, you must shift your mindset. Instead of asking, 'Why is this happening to me?' start asking, 'What is this trying to teach me?' This shift in perspective transforms adversity from something that victimizes you into something that empowers you. It allows you to extract meaning from struggle and use it as a stepping stone toward success.

Remember, overcoming adversity does not mean you will never struggle again. Life will continue to present challenges. But each time you face adversity and push through it, you build confidence in your ability to handle whatever comes your way. You are not defined by what happens to you. You are defined by how you respond. Use your struggles as fuel for your transformation, and watch how your life begins to shift in ways you never imagined.

Self-Mastery: The Ultimate Transformation

True transformation is not just about changing your circumstances—it is about mastering yourself. Self-mastery is the highest form of personal development. It is the ability to control your thoughts, emotions, and actions in alignment with your goals and values. It means becoming the conscious architect of your life rather than being a passive participant.

Self-mastery requires deep self-awareness. It is about knowing who you are, what drives you, what triggers you, and what holds you back. Many people live their lives on autopilot, reacting to circumstances rather than shaping them. Mastering yourself means taking full responsibility for your actions, habits, and mindset.

One of the most critical aspects of self-mastery is emotional intelligence. How often do we let our emotions dictate our decisions? Anger, fear, insecurity, and self-doubt can cloud our judgment and keep us stuck. When you master your emotions, you do not suppress them—you learn to understand and channel them in a productive manner. You become the calm in the storm rather than being swept away by it.

Another critical element of self-mastery is discipline. Success in any area of life—whether personal, professional, or spiritual—demands consistency. It is not about motivation, which fluctuates, but about the discipline to show up every day and do what needs to be done, regardless of how you feel. Discipline is what separates those who achieve lasting transformation from those who remain stuck in cycles of unfulfilled potential.

Self-mastery does not mean perfection. It means becoming a student of yourself, constantly learning, evolving, and improving. The more you master yourself, the more control you have over your destiny. You are no longer at the mercy of circumstances—you become the force that shapes your life. When you commit to self-mastery, you unlock a power within you that is limitless. The external world will always have challenges, but when you master yourself, you gain the tools to navigate anything life throws your way with confidence and resilience. Transformation begins the moment you decide to take control of yourself. The journey to self-mastery is lifelong, but every step brings you closer to the person you were always meant to be.

Final Thoughts: The Power of Betting on Yourself

If there is one truth that has been woven through every step of transformation, it is this: you must bet on yourself. No one else will take a greater chance on you than you will. No one else can walk the path meant for you. And no one else can decide to rise, to change, to break free from the constraints of the past and embrace the limitless potential that lies ahead.

Betting on yourself is not about arrogance—it is about self-trust. It's about knowing that you are worthy, capable, and have everything within you to create the life you desire. It means refusing to wait for external validation, refusing to shrink yourself to fit someone else's expectations, and refusing to let fear dictate your choices.

So many people live their lives playing it safe, waiting for permission, waiting for the "right time," waiting for someone else to believe in them before they believe in themselves. But waiting will only keep you stagnant. Transformation requires boldness. It requires a leap of faith. It requires you to look in the mirror and say, I am the author of my own story. I choose to create my destiny.

The path of self-betting is not always easy. You will encounter resistance. People will doubt you. You may even doubt yourself at times. But here's the secret: every great achiever, every visionary, every individual who has transformed their life had to bet on themselves first. They had to believe in their vision before anyone else did. They had to be willing to fail forward, learn, grow, and push through the discomfort of uncertainty.

To honestly bet on yourself, you must commit to the following:

- **Trust Your Intuition**: You already know what you are meant to do. Stop second-guessing yourself. Listen to that inner voice and follow through on it.

- **Invest in Your Growth**: Whether it's time, money, or energy, invest in becoming the best version of yourself. Take courses, read books, seek mentorship—whatever it takes to elevate your mindset and skill set.

- **Refuse to Settle**: You were not born to live a life of mediocrity. Push beyond your comfort zone and dare to create a life that excites you.

- **Take Ownership**: No more excuses. No more blaming circumstances or people. You are responsible for your outcomes. Take full accountability for your actions and choices.

- **Persevere Relentlessly**: There will be setbacks. There will be moments of doubt. However, if you persist and refuse to quit, success will become inevitable.

When you bet on yourself, you activate a force greater than fear. You awaken the unstoppable power of belief. You begin to move with conviction, make decisions with clarity, and walk in alignment with your purpose. The world does not reward hesitation—it rewards courage, action, and unwavering belief. The proof of that power? It lives in the moments we never forget—the ones that branded our soul and built our backbone.

I will never forget the day I stood there—pregnant, broke, betrayed, and barely holding it together—being told I had to leave the only shelter I had. I can still feel the sting of that moment. The silent heartbreak. The quiet vow. I didn't cry. I *decided*. Right there, in that small room heavy with disappointment and generational silence, I stood up in my soul. Not because I had it all figured out, but because I realized no one was coming to save me. And in that realization, I found my power. I wasn't just being pushed out of a house—I was being pushed into destiny.

So when the call came when the door cracked open through Ms. Denise, I didn't walk—I *ran*. And with every class I took, every paycheck I earned, and every skill I mastered, I was rebuilding what life had tried to tear down. Not just for me but for every little girl who's ever been told she wasn't worth fighting for. I am proof that you can be dismissed, discarded, and doubted—and still rise. That moment was my revolution. And I hope, as you turn this page, you realize—you hold that same power, too.

My transformation started that day. The decision to reclaim my power helped me build not just a life but multiple 7-figure businesses. Today, every client I coach, every woman I help rise, is fueled by that same fire that once lit up my darkest hour. That's the gift of transformation—it doesn't just change *you*; it gives you the authority to change *others*.

Now that you've read my story, I want to challenge *you*. Let this be *your* defining moment. Don't allow anyone to take your voice. Don't allow anyone to shape your future. You get to choose. You get to declare that today—*right now*—is the day you stop surviving and start reclaiming your power. Don't wait for permission. Make the decision. And then... let your transformation begin. From this moment forward, bet on yourself unapologetically. Dare to dream bigger than you ever have before. And then take bold, relentless action to bring those dreams to life. Because at the end of the day, the only thing standing between you and the life you desire is the decision to believe in yourself. Make that decision. Make it now. And never look back.

HIT THE MARK

- Your past does not define you—your response to it does.

- Freedom and growth begin with internal work.

- Self-mastery is the highest form of transformation. When you lead yourself with discipline and emotional intelligence, your external world adjusts to match your inner world.

- The most sacred decision you can make? Betting on yourself.

Reflection

Transformation isn't a trend. It's a choice. And you don't need permission to begin.

Kymberly Givens

8
A WOMAN TRUCKING
With Gratitude & Resilience

Dear Self, *Is this my life right now?*

I'm 45, single, and striving to fulfill my dream of becoming my own boss. You'd be proud of me. I've overcome many setbacks, but I'm still here. I'm the only sibling out of six children who followed in my father's footsteps by becoming a truck driver. I'm a proud female truck driver! My father always said, "You'll know when you find your passion. It will feel different in a way you can't put into words." I have found mine, and now I am learning how to turn my passion into a profitable venture.

The journey to discovery hasn't been easy, and I didn't always know this was what I wanted. I have worked in many different sectors. But after years of countless job changes—retail, EMT, CNA, MOA, warehouse, and call center representative—I knew it was time to stop making someone else's bank account grow and start investing in myself. On June 10, 2007, my life changed in ways I could never have imagined. This was the day I stepped out of my comfort zone to challenge myself. Little did I know that the burning desire in me to do more would become the catalyst that would direct me to my passion. Life has a way of guiding us to our purpose, and if we pay attention, we'll end up exactly where we need to be. That wasn't a lesson I understood at the time, but it was one I would learn over the years.

I remember the overwhelming nervousness that washed over me as I stood there, questioning myself: Was I making the right decision? Could I do this? The fear of the unknown was gripping, and I wondered if I was setting myself up for failure. But at that moment, everything changed. The transportation director at the school district interviewed me, and in what felt like the blink of an eye, he offered me the job on the spot. I couldn't believe it. I was in complete shock, and as I walked back to the car, where my dad and son were waiting, I could barely process what had just happened. The doubt, the fear, the uncertainty, they all seemed to vanish in an instant. It was one of those rare, life-changing moments when I realized that I had just taken a giant leap, and somehow, it all came together. My heart raced with excitement and disbelief, and I felt this wave of pride and hope for what was to come next.

That was my first CDL position, and let me tell you, I was scared out of my mind. How was I going to drive something so big, something that felt like it could swallow the road whole? My first job was driving a school bus, and I remember feeling the weight of that responsibility. But despite the fear, a deep sense of excitement ran through me. The thought of driving—of being in control of such a massive machine—was both thrilling and intimidating. I passed my road test, received my white envelope, and walked into the DMV to obtain my Commercial Driver's License Class B (CDL-B). I'll never forget that moment. It wasn't just a piece of paper; it was the key to a new chapter of my life. It ignited something inside me—a fire that would push me to aim higher. I knew then that I wasn't going to stop just driving a school bus. I wanted to challenge myself to obtain my Class A CDL, a license that would allow me to drive any vehicle with wheels, and that became my next goal.

I loved my job. I loved the open road, the hum of the engine beneath me, and the responsibility that came with transporting children to school, ensuring they were safe and ready to learn. My job felt like it was so much more than just driving—it was about shaping their day, about being part of something bigger than myself. Despite my love for it, life had other plans, and I experienced a new reality—setback after success. After five years, I was wrongfully terminated. That hit me hard. Hurt, shame, depression, and any other emotion that equated my life to a failure--all came flooding in. I began to wonder if I had lost my passion for driving. I began to wonder if maybe this wasn't for me anymore. I felt lost. The very thing I thought I was meant to do was suddenly taken away from me. It was a punch to the gut that left me doubting myself and my future.

However, something unexpected happened that changed everything. God used a sign to show me that I hadn't missed my calling. I was just being rerouted. That day, I picked up my son from school, and as we were driving home, he pointed to a semi-tractor truck on the road.

'Ma,' he said, 'I can't wait until you get your truck so I can sit up high and look down at everyone as we drive by them.'

At that moment, something inside of me clicked. I was overwhelmed with emotion. My heart felt full. I pulled over to the side of the road, hugged him tightly, and let the tears flow. He saw me crying and wondered what he had done to cause such a reaction. I explained to him that those were tears of happiness. That moment was a clear sign from God, a reminder that my passion for driving was far from gone—it was still very much alive. It was just buried under disappointment. My son, in his simple way, spoke words that reignited a dream I thought I had lost. I decided to keep going, and this time, I would go even bigger.

In May 2012, I graduated from York Technical Professional Truck Driving School with my Class A CDL, hitting another goal I had set for myself. But I didn't stop there. It was time to set a new one. One afternoon, after a nap, it was as if a light bulb went off in my mind—I suddenly had a dream of becoming my own boss and running my own trucking company. The idea of owning my own business was both exciting and daunting. I had no roadmap, no blueprint, just a desire to break free from the limitations of working for someone else.

Most people think starting a business is easy. But in reality, it takes an immense amount of discipline and dedication. I continue to work full-time as a CDL driver trainer and safety coordinator while building my business. Balancing both roles, especially with 14-hour night shifts and only getting 6 to 7 hours of sleep, is exhausting. But I keep going. Eric Thomas once said, "When you want to succeed as bad as you want to breathe, then you'll be successful."

Becoming an entrepreneur requires more than just hard work. It requires mental fortitude. It requires the strength to push forward, even when every part of you wants to quit. There will be days when your business isn't making any money, and you'll wonder if it's all worth it. But you have to keep going, even when it's hard. You must continue to invest in your business and yourself, even when the results aren't immediate. **Entrepreneurship is not for the faint of heart—it's for those with the courage to push through obstacles and keep climbing.** Life will throw everything it can at you, and you will have every reason to quit. But if you quit, you will never discover what you are capable of.

Here's what I've learned: every step, jump, setback, and challenge is part of the process. It's all necessary for growth. This is my journey, and it's been far from easy. From facing physical illness to seeing my children struggle with mental health to forgiving those who wronged me—life hasn't been a smooth ride. But through it all, I rise. The label of being the "strong one" is not without its challenges, but I wear it with pride because it means I've overcome. I hope my story will inspire you to roll up your sleeves, pull up your bootstraps, and give your all to your dreams. "Because sometimes the scariest leaps lead to the most beautiful flights." As someone still on the road to success, don't compare your journey to anyone else's. It's easy to get caught up in other people's success stories, but the truth is, they probably struggled too. The key is to stay inspired, not discouraged. Focus on your journey, even when it feels challenging or uncertain.

What keeps me going is the vision of my future. I see it every day. I know that one day, my trucking company will make me a wealthy person. I know it because I can see it clearly in my mind—every time I look at my truck parked outside, I'm reminded of why I'm doing this. Owning my truck is my motivation. It fuels me to keep going, no matter what the obstacles are. I've taught myself that every small success is worth celebrating.

My journey is not the perfect success story that people often expect, but it's real. It's raw. It's gritty. But it's mine, and it's full of gratitude and resilience. Looking back, it hasn't been easy, but I'm doing something that most people only talk about—dream of doing but never actually take action on. I started this journey with nothing but a dream, and today, I own my truck. The title is in my hand, and that's a massive win for me.

You are Powerful!

One day, I woke up early, turned on a motivational video, and as I listened, something deep inside me shifted. The words resonated with my soul, and I began speaking affirmations aloud as I walked through my house. In those few minutes, it hit me—I am capable of amazing things. I am more powerful than I give myself credit for. I am the one responsible for creating the life I want. And the question that followed was, "Where do I go from here?"

Listening to that video and reflecting on my journey up until that point, I knew one thing for sure: I had to act now. If I wanted to get back on track and fulfill my dreams, I needed to take charge of my future. If you want to build your dreams, you have to be so passionate and so driven that nothing can stop you. It's not easy, and if it were, everyone would be doing it. But here's the thing: this is why I keep building, even when I feel unsupported. I wake up and move forward, even when my bank account is telling me to turn back.

But quitting? That was never an option.

So, I changed directions. I decided to find my path in the trucking industry by starting as a dispatcher for owner-operators. I dove in headfirst—learning the ins and outs of the industry, taking the necessary courses, and investing in myself. Even when the results weren't immediate, I continued to push forward. I spent countless hours talking to truck drivers, often sacrificing sleep, convincing them that I could dispatch for them while still working my full-time job. And I'll admit—there were times when I wanted to give up. There were days when it felt like nothing was working. But I refused to stop.

Is this you right now? Are you in a place where everything feels off track, but you know deep down that you're not ready to quit? Even on my worst days, I refuse to give up. Because I've learned this: when it feels impossible, the only way forward is to keep going. And if I can do it, so can you! If you find yourself in a situation where nothing seems to be going right, remain determined to move forward. I've been there. I refuse to quit because I know that the only way through is to keep going. Even when it feels impossible, pushing forward is the only option.

The raw truth is that success can be a lonely road. I know what it's like to bootstrap and face rejection after rejection. Starting a small trucking business with no capital is incredibly stressful! I applied for countless grants and loans, hoping to get a chance, but I kept hearing "No" repeatedly. Voicemails, emails, phone calls—no matter what I did, I couldn't get anyone to give me a shot. Post-COVID, the world was beginning to return to normal, yet door after door kept closing. It was devastating. Day after day, week after week, I heard the same thing: No. No. No.

But I refused to give up. I invested in myself, taking classes and learning everything I could. I spent hours talking with truck drivers, even when I should have been sleeping, trying to convince them that I could dispatch for them while working my full-time job. There were days when I felt like throwing in the towel. I spent a significant amount of money and time setting up KLD Transport LLC, but still—nothing. It felt like I was stuck in a loop.

But then I remembered why I had started and why I had chosen this path.

There were times when I had to take a break. The journey started to mess with my mental health, and it became overwhelming. I had to place something in plain sight that reminded me of my why. This will not be an easy journey. When doubt creeps in, go back to your "why." It'll help get you back on track when you feel like quitting. I encourage you to do the same.

You can't give up on yourself. You are the reason to keep going. When I feel overwhelmed, I pray for strength and encourage myself to persevere. I also started setting small goals and checking them off one by one instead of trying to do everything all at once.

Learning from your failures is the best lesson you'll ever get. It teaches you not to be ashamed of them but to embrace them. Every challenge became a lesson. Every rough patch built my resilience. It wasn't easy, but I began to trust myself more. I began making more intelligent decisions and stopped expecting quick wins. I knew if I could push through this, someone else out there could too. If you continue on your journey, even when it gets tough, and never give up, you'll be incredibly proud of who you become and what you achieve on your own.

After a few months, I realized it was time to get back into the game. I also added another stream of income while my trucking business was slow. One night, I hopped on YouTube and watched a video by Noelle Randall, in which she discussed how to grow your wealth. Feeling inspired by her message, I made an impulsive decision to book a ticket to Orlando, FL, for the Grow Your Wealth Conference—during hurricane season. And yes, Hurricane Helene made landfall while I was there. Talk about timing!

At the time, I was convinced that adding another stream of income was the key, and once again, God showed me favor in a way that would guide my next steps. The turnaround didn't come in a big, dramatic moment, but rather, it came quietly. It was moments that would've been easy to overlook, but I paid attention. One evening, I was scrolling through Facebook Marketplace, just browsing, when I saw a 2014 Freightliner truck listed by someone I knew. I immediately texted them about it, and before I knew it, we had negotiated the price, and I sent my deposit.

This small victory was just the motivation I needed to refocus on KLD Transport LLC. I started the business in January 2022 without a truck, but after almost two years, I was finally able to acquire my first truck. I cannot explain the feeling when you work so hard to build something from scratch, and then you finally see it paying off. It wasn't a huge, flashy moment, but it was one of those quiet, personal victories. Sitting back in silence, with a big smile on my face and a heart full of joy, knowing that my hard work, gratitude, and resilience were finally making things move forward.

After the conference, I returned home with a renewed mindset, ready to start a new venture: Carolina Priority Solutions LLC, a real estate investment business. However, just as things were looking up, I received an email from my insurance company in February 2025, stating that they had terminated my coverage for the Freightliner semi-truck because they deemed it too risky, without any prior warning.

Another setback. But rather than getting discouraged, I decided to take a step back, strategize, and find an alternative approach. I got a job to bring in some income while I figured out how to make this truck start generating cash flow. It was another challenge, but I knew it was just another part of the journey.

I've been told by many people that I am the epitome of resilience, and as I reflect on my life's journey, filled with struggles and challenges, I now understand what they see that I couldn't see for myself. You see, gratitude is the quality of being thankful, the readiness to show appreciation and to return kindness. It's a positive force that can transform your life every single day. No one day is ever the same. Be grateful for the small victories because huge victories are on the way if you keep pushing forward, no matter the obstacles, struggles, or setbacks.

Always choose gratitude over complaints. Embrace failure, closed doors, and the challenges—because they are all a part of the process to get where you need to be in life. When you start to hear praise and acknowledgment from people you know and from those you don't, it hits you in a way words can't describe. It confirmed everything I had second-guessed about myself.

To you, my friend, I say: Get up and begin your journey! In those moments when I received recognition, I couldn't help but get emotional—tears filled my eyes. It made me realize that this was bigger than my dreams, but in such a beautiful way. I'm not just building small businesses. I'm showing people like you that it's possible. You don't need to have it all figured out.

If you're in that middle space right now—where things feel slow, and you're wondering if all your effort is making a difference—hold on. Things are about to shift in your favor. Stay the course and wait. You're doing something right; things are falling into place the way they should. Keep grinding, keep pressing on, and hold fast to your faith. If there's one thing I've learned on this journey, it's that success doesn't belong to the smartest, the most connected, or the most prepared. It belongs to the ones who keep going, no matter what.

Becoming your own boss isn't easy, but the process will teach you invaluable life lessons along the way. You can be scared, uncertain, and imperfect—and still go for it. Little by little, the mountain starts to build. I stopped second-guessing myself and began making more confident decisions. Things were starting to grow, and as I often say to my plants,

"It's Happening!"

I've had other owners reach out to me, sharing information to help me grow and introducing me to other trucking business owners. But make no mistake, this was favor—God's favor, I say. Some might call it luck, but I know that luck has nothing to do with it when you have the favor of the Most High and your guardian angels watching over you. Always remember this and keep it in your spirit: "What God has for you, it is for you."

You see, God saw all those late nights, early mornings, every tear that fell, and every door that closed. And I'm still pushing forward, even though it's so easy to stop and give up. But the best part? As I'm writing this, I'm sharing my story to inspire you to keep going. I am so proud of how far I've come, and I want you to know that you can do it, too. Your journey may look different from mine but know this: sharing it will help someone else. Let the world see what you've worked so hard to build because it's part of your brand.

Most people can't go through hell and come out stronger than they were when they went in. That's the part of the journey no one tells you about. The biggest win isn't cash flow—because, honestly, I don't have it yet—or even all the milestones. The biggest win is the version of you that believed in the dream, that believed it could be real and made it happen.

Friend, if you've made it this far into my story, I hope I've given you enough proof to start—and to keep going. You don't need to have it all figured out before you start your business. You need to start your journey.

You are allowed to be a beginner and still believe in your success.

You are allowed to grow slowly.

You are allowed to be scared and still move forward.

I have faith in ME! Building my faith gave me the fuel to keep going when I had to search for another way. When one way didn't work, faith helped me turn setbacks into stepping stones. Faith reminded me that I don't have to be perfect; I have to be present.

You are Capable.

You are Worthy.

You are Ready.

Not someday—*Right Now!*

Don't wait until you're qualified. Don't wait until every step is mapped out; instead, take action. Don't wait until the fear disappears. Start with what you know. Start with what you have. Start where you are in life. Because one day, someone will look at you and say, "Your journey gave me the courage to start my own."

And that's when you'll realize your journey wasn't just about starting a business—it was about building the version of yourself that didn't give up, that kept going even when it was hard. You will see that person you worked so hard to become—the one who grew, built, and overcame—and you'll know that you didn't just build a business. You built yourself. You don't have to have all the answers to get started. Just a little faith. A little fire. And a whole lot of believing in yourself.

I've had many setbacks along the way, and I'm still working on landing my first trucking contract. But I'm not giving up! Stay tuned—this story isn't over. It's okay to cry, to feel upset—but don't stay there. Get up and find another way. There's always another way.

You have to find it. And if you can't find it, create your way!

HIT THE MARK

- Your beginning doesn't disqualify your becoming. You can be the "strong one" and still need support.

- Setbacks aren't stop signs. They're signposts directing you to adjust, not quit.

- It's okay to cry. To pause. To start again. What matters is that you keep going.

- You're allowed to grow slowly, start messy, and believe in yourself loudly.

Reflection

You've been building silently, grinding faithfully, and believing—even when no one else did. You are not behind. You're right on time. Keep going.

Jennifer McPhail

9
THE GIFT OF EXPECTATION

Starting a business requires a pioneering spirit. You're heading into unfamiliar territory with nothing but a vision, some grit, and the belief that you can build something where nothing exists yet. As a real estate investor and a business owner with a disability, I know that the path isn't always paved or accessible — sometimes you have to build the road yourself. But that's what pioneers do: they move forward anyway, adapting, problem-solving, and refusing to wait for perfect conditions. Success doesn't come from waiting at the edge — it comes from pushing in and claiming your ground. Owning a business is a huge adventure that is both exciting and challenging.

Writing this chapter has given me space to reflect on what it takes to succeed as a person with a disability in a world that wasn't built for us. We come from every background, every community, every walk of life. But there's one trait I've seen again and again in every successful person with a disability I know: relentlessness. It's the refusal to give up, even when the road gets hard. It's the stubborn insistence that we deserve to be here. It's the quiet determination to keep pushing forward, even when others tell us to sit down.

The day I was born, the doctors told my parents not to get attached. "She won't make it through the night," they said. "Don't even name her." But my mom? She wasn't about to let me fight alone.

That night, she snuck into the NICU, pulled up a chair, and sat by my side, holding my tiny hand through the incubator. She stayed all night, refusing to leave me for even a moment. It was then, I believe, that love was cemented—not just in the womb, but beyond it. Her love enveloped me, anchored me, and carried me through those fragile first hours. Even as a newborn, I believe I felt it—the warmth of her presence, the strength of her refusal to let go. Babies may not understand words, but they know when someone is fighting for them. They know when they are loved. Her love was the first shelter I ever knew. It gave me the strength to keep breathing, to keep fighting, from my very first breath.

We survived the hospital scare, and against all odds, I pulled through. I'd won my first battle, but my health challenges were far from over. By the time I was a toddler and still hadn't spoken, doctors told my parents I would probably never talk—that they should consider institutionalizing me. Their response was the same—it was never an option to give up. When the doctors gave up on me, my parents pushed even harder. Where others saw limits, they saw possibilities. They weren't willing to accept a future where I couldn't communicate, couldn't learn, or couldn't belong. They believed there had to be a way.

They turned their hope into action, determined to break through the silence. My mom created a homemade picture book, using shapes and textures to teach me words. She and my dad spent hours every day trying to help me communicate. Nothing seemed to work—until one day, while my mom was cleaning, she heard my voice from the dining room. I was tracing a penny with my baby sister and said,

"Look, baby Penny," I copied exactly what my parents had done with me.

It was my first spoken sentence—and proof that I was learning, even if I couldn't show it yet. My parents were my first advocates. Long before I could speak for myself, they spoke up for me. Before I could fight for myself, they fought for me. And maybe—without even realizing it—they planted the seeds of advocacy deep inside me.

They showed me what it looked like to stand up for myself and others, to push back, to believe in someone's potential when others only saw limitations. Their fight for me became the foundation of my fight for others because I've learned that a single person's belief, a single person's fight, can change the entire trajectory of a life.

Around that same time, Section 504 of the Rehabilitation Act was passed, requiring federally funded programs and buildings to be accessible to people with disabilities. There was a growing movement to enforce these rights, but for families like mine, it was still an uphill battle. While my parents were fighting for me at home, a broader fight for disability rights was unfolding across the country—one that would shape the opportunities available to me as I grew up.

I entered elementary school as one of the first kids with disabilities integrated into a regular classroom. Most children like me were automatically placed in special education, regardless of their abilities. But my parents fought for me. On the first day of school, I was proudly wearing my new outfit. I picked a desk and sat down, excited to learn. However, the teacher then called me over. She stapled a note to my shirt and read, "This doesn't belong in my classroom."

That note lit a fire in me. It was my first "rage cry." I showed it to my homeroom teacher and later brought it home to my parents. That night, my mom sat me down and gave me a choice: I could stay in the easier, more comfortable homeroom class, or I could take the more challenging spelling class—the one where I'd learn more but face more obstacles.

I didn't hesitate.

"She should be fired," I told my mom. "It's not fair."

My mom agreed—but gently explained that some of the teacher's bosses thought she was right. She told me the truth: I'd face bullies. I'd face people who underestimated me simply because I was different. But no matter what, she, my dad, and my homeroom teacher would always have my back.

I chose the more challenging class.

That teacher tested me every day, failing me for the slightest mistake—forgetting to dot an "i" or cross a "t." Before the final exam, my parents sat with me for hours as I wrote every spelling word 100 times. My little sister, just five or six years old, stayed by my side as well. By the end of the year, the bully who'd taunted me the most was the one who admitted I belonged in that classroom.

That year, I also learned to use a wheelchair. My right arm was weaker than my left, so I spent much time going in circles until I built the strength to push straight. As the school year drew to a close, I was strong enough to compete with the other kids on the annual track and field day. Not only did I compete, I won two first-place ribbons and a third-place ribbon. A deep sense of pride and accomplishment washed over me after placing in track and field. In that moment, it solidified something I would carry with me for life: there's nothing I can't do when I set my mind to it.

That victory wasn't just about ribbons—it was a declaration. It proved to me and everyone watching that my wheelchair wasn't a limitation. It was simply part of how I moved through the world. Every step forward made me stronger, not just physically, but mentally as well. That day gave me confidence that I would draw from again and again whenever life threw obstacles in my path.

It taught me that success isn't about having an easy journey—it's about having the determination to finish the race, no matter how hard the course.

We moved to Bastrop for a fresh start after my parents separated. That was a new experience in small-town life—raising goats and horses on a big property. My favorite horse was Sonny, a golden palomino too wild to ride. I loved him for his independent spirit. He was always gentle with me as if he understood I was different. Maybe animals know.

Eventually, we had to move into an apartment, and I became the only student in Bastrop who used a wheelchair. That wasn't always easy. At an age when most kids want to fit in, I had to learn how to stand out—and be proud of it. I didn't want people only to see my wheelchair. I wanted them to see me. As I was growing up, the world around me was also changing. The fight for disability rights wasn't just happening in protests or courtrooms—it was shaping the very spaces we live in. Laws were being passed that would impact not only where I could go but how I could live. While I was learning to navigate school hallways in my wheelchair, activists were working tirelessly to ensure that those hallways—and eventually, our homes—would be welcoming to people with disabilities like me.

Living in a world not built with accessibility in mind is not only inconvenient but it is also dangerous and it isolates us. Humans are pack animals. It is impossible to have a healthy sense of self without a healthy sense of community. For 32 years, I dedicated myself to community organizing with ADAPT, a disability rights organization. I loved every minute of it. Advocacy wasn't just my work—it was my identity, my calling, my way of making the world a little more just. It demands a great deal from you. You give your talents, your resources and your time. In return, it teaches you to lead, challenges you to step out of your comfort zone and encourages you to learn new things. One of the most essential gifts my time as a community organizer gave me was the chance to stand out because of who I am, not how I present myself. When I am on my own among nondisabled people, the description can be, "You know, the one in the wheelchair." That is not possible when there are 200 people in wheelchairs. I loved every minute of it. Advocacy wasn't just my work—it was my identity, my calling, my way of making the world a little more just.

But then, something changed.

During the COVID-19 pandemic, I needed a new wheelchair. The chair I was provided wasn't just uncomfortable—it was unusable. It didn't fit my body. It couldn't be adjusted. It left me trapped. Everyone agreed: I needed a different model. But because my insurance only covers one wheelchair every five years, there was no clear path forward.

Suddenly, the freedom I'd fought so hard for—the ability to move, to work, to show up—was stripped away. I found myself facing a new kind of advocacy: the fight to reclaim my independence. I worked with my vocational rehabilitation counselor. We explored every option. But no matter how we tried, the system was stacked against me.

Without a chair that fit, I couldn't continue my work as a community organizer. The thing I loved most had become out of reach. And so, for the first time in decades, I had to ask myself: What now? How can I continue to advocate for change while also establishing security for myself? How can I create a future that allows me to live on my terms as I age?

I realized that if I wanted to stay independent, I couldn't wait for the system to catch up. I had to build my safety net. And so, I made a decision I never expected: I became an entrepreneur. I never intended to become a business owner. What started as a personal decision quickly became something bigger. As I took my first steps into entrepreneurship, I realized I wasn't just building a business for myself—I was confronting the very systems that had failed me and many others like me. For many years, I'd relied on home health aides and community-based support programs to live independently. Yet the irony is apparent: institutional care is fully funded and guaranteed by the government, while programs that help people like me stay in our own homes are optional, underfunded, and constantly under threat.

The system is broken, with people like me paying the price every day. In many ways, this is the best time in history to be a person with a disability. We've made incredible progress. We've passed laws. We've changed our policies. And yet, despite all that, I still often find myself the only disabled person in the room as I navigate the world of business ownership. Why? Because there are still too many barriers blocking our path. Physical barriers. Systemic barriers. Attitudinal barriers. Barriers that whisper, "This isn't for you."

When I decided to start my business, I expected a few people to question my choice. What I didn't expect was how many people tried to talk me out of it. I lost count of how many well-meaning voices told me to stick with what I knew, to play it safe, and to accept my limitations.

But I kept going.

Today, as the owner and manager of McPhail Enterprises LLC, I'm building something bigger than a business. I'm investing in accessible housing for others, creating opportunities, and filling gaps that the system ignores. And in doing so, I'm building a safety net for myself—a way to stay independent, secure, and in control of my future. The skills I'm using every day—persistence, creative problem-solving, and advocacy—aren't new. They're the same skills I started developing as a little girl, tracing a penny in a photo album. They're the same tools I used to survive: teachers who said I didn't belong, classrooms that weren't designed for me, and systems that tried to push me aside.

That's why we decided to call this chapter "The Gift of Expectation." Because the greatest gift my parents gave me wasn't protection; it wasn't pity. It wasn't lowering the bar to make things easier. It was this simple, powerful truth: You are expected to work hard. You are expected to do your best. You are expected to succeed. They didn't tell me what I couldn't do. They taught me what I could.

And today, I carry that expectation forward—not just for myself, but for everyone who's ever been told they don't belong. For every child, tracing shapes in a photo album. Every young person dreams of a future they're not sure they're allowed to have, and every disabled entrepreneur wonders if there's room for them at the table.

I want them to know that there is. And if there's not? We'll build our table.

This phase of my life coincided with a significant milestone in disability rights: the passing and implementation of the Fair Housing Act Amendments. This law required that newly built multifamily housing constructed after March 31, 1991, be designed to accommodate people with disabilities. It meant that accessible routes, adaptable units on the first floor, and accessible common areas, such as leasing offices, mailboxes, and playgrounds, were no longer optional—they were required by law.

For example, bathrooms in these units needed to provide enough space for a wheelchair to turn around, include reinforcements for installing grab bars, and ensure that sinks, light switches, outlets, and thermostats were placed within reach. Most people never think about how vital these details are—until they need them. The Fair Housing Act also guarantees the right to request reasonable modifications and accommodations to make a home livable.

Then, in 1990, another landmark victory arrived: the passage of the Americans with Disabilities Act (ADA). For the first time, a comprehensive law addressed access across public accommodations, transportation, employment, communications, and state and local government programs. The ADA was—and still is—a game changer. It felt like living two lifetimes: my life before the ADA and my life after it. But while it transformed access to public spaces, it didn't guarantee accessibility inside private homes. The fight for accessible housing wasn't over.

The Fight for Accessible Housing

I hope these stories—and these laws—help underline a powerful lesson: we must never settle for less than we deserve. That's why accessible housing is so critical. Home is where we let our guard down. It's where we build relationships, raise families, and dream big. However, when a home isn't accessible, it becomes a barrier rather than a refuge.

That's why I'm passionate about promoting a concept called visitability—the idea that basic accessibility features should be built into every home, even single-family houses. Visitability encompasses features such as a zero-step entrance, an accessible bathroom on the main floor, sufficient clear space for a wheelchair to maneuver, reinforced walls for grab bars, and accessible outlets and controls.

People often don't realize how quickly a disability or simply aging can change what a home needs. A broken leg, an aging parent, an unexpected diagnosis—suddenly, stairs, narrow hallways, and inaccessible bathrooms become major obstacles.

Building homes with visitability in mind isn't just about disability rights; it's about future-proofing our communities so no one gets left behind. It also makes economic sense. Accessible homes increase in value, lower renovation costs in the long run, and enable people to age in place instead of moving into expensive institutional care. Equally as important, visitability also makes it possible for people with mobility impairments to visit family, friends, and neighbors. We will be able to trick or treat, enjoy holiday meals, or have a cup of coffee with our neighbors.

According to a 2023 study by the U.S. Department of Housing and Urban Development, less than 1% of housing in the U.S. is accessible to people with disabilities. That's not just a statistic—it's a daily challenge for people like me when we try to find housing. This shortage doesn't just inconvenience people with disabilities—it forces many into institutional settings. Right now, nearly 900,000 Americans under 64 live in nursing homes or similar facilities, not because they need intensive care but because they can't find an affordable, accessible place to live.

This lack of housing limits independence, strains families, and puts pressure on our healthcare system. As our population ages, the need for accessible homes is expected to grow. Between 2010 and 2020, the U.S. population aged 65 and older grew by nearly 39%, from 40 million to 56 million. By 2050, that number is expected to rise to 82 million—nearly a quarter of the population. Yet even as the need rises, a 2019 HUD report found that nearly 40% of households that include someone with a disability live in homes that aren't accessible.

We can do better. We must do better.

Building accessible communities doesn't just meet a legal standard—it builds a moral one. Every time we create an accessible space, we give the next generation the gift of expectation. We teach them they belong. We show them that they have the right to live fully, independently, and with dignity.

When I think back to that moment in the classroom—the teacher stapling a note to my shirt, telling me I didn't belong—I realize now how defining that day was. I was just a little girl in a new outfit, excited to learn. But in an instant, I discovered that some people would see my wheelchair before they saw me. I could've let that moment crush me. I could've accepted her judgment. But instead, I felt something rise inside me: a determination not to let her—or anyone—decide my future.

That was my first real fight. And what I didn't understand then was that it wouldn't be my last. That fight prepared me for every closed door, every low expectation, every system that tried to box me in. It was in those uncomfortable, unfair moments that I discovered what I was made of.

I've come to believe that the very things we struggle with—the places where we feel disadvantaged or different—are often the places where our purpose is waiting. Our discomfort holds clues to our calling. Every time I was pushed aside or underestimated, I had a choice: to rise or to shrink. To fight or to fold. I chose to rise. I chose to speak up. I chose to become an advocate, not just for myself, but for others who couldn't speak for themselves.

Before you turn the page, I want to leave you with a challenge. I want you to take a closer look at the places in your life—or in your community—where you see injustice, inequality, or inaccessibility. Where are the barriers that too many people have learned to accept quietly? What doors are still closed? What tables are still missing chairs?

Maybe those gaps aren't just problems waiting for someone else to solve. Maybe they're signs pointing you toward your purpose.

Ask yourself:

Where could I be showing up more boldly?

Where am I holding back when I've been called to step up?

Who have I been called to advocate for?

Whose voice could I help amplify?

We don't all have to start a business or lead a protest to make a difference. Sometimes advocacy looks like speaking up in a meeting, making room for someone else, challenging a harmful policy, or mentoring the next generation. Sometimes, advocacy doesn't look like leading a march or writing new legislation. Sometimes, advocacy is quiet. Personal. Everyday. Sometimes, it looks like speaking up in a meeting when someone's voice is being overlooked. It's using your influence to say, "Let's hear from her." It's noticing who's not in the room and asking why, and then working to open the door.

Sometimes, advocacy means making room for someone else to shine, even if it means stepping aside for a moment. It's mentoring a young person who reminds you of yourself. It's pulling up another chair at the table or even building a longer table so more can fit.

Sometimes, advocacy means challenging a harmful policy, even if it doesn't affect you directly. It's recognizing that injustice anywhere threatens justice everywhere. It's standing with someone whose struggle you may never fully understand—but showing up anyway because no one should have to fight alone.

Sometimes, advocacy is teaching. Listening. Or even giving someone the tools they need to advocate for themselves. Sometimes, it's the example they never thought they'd see—a person who looks like them, moves like them, talks like them, leads, builds, and thrives.

Advocacy doesn't have to be loud to be powerful. It just has to be consistent. Courageous. Willing to use what you have, where you are, to make things better for someone else. Whatever it looks like for you, know this: your voice matters. Your actions matter. Your willingness to stand up, speak up, and show up matters. And in doing so, you just might be offering someone else the gift of expectation—the belief that they, too, are worthy of being seen, heard, and included.

HIT THE MARK

- You don't need perfect conditions to move forward—you need to stop waiting and start building.

- The road to business, advocacy, or leadership may not be paved for you, but that doesn't mean you can't achieve success.

- Real change happens not just in courtrooms and campaigns but also in classrooms, home offices, and through challenging conversations.

Reflection

You don't need anyone's permission to take up space. You are not just welcome—you are needed.

Mercedes Sanchez

IN THE RING OF LIFE

They say pressure makes diamonds—if that's true, I've been forged under fire.

My name is Mercedes Sanchez, and I am the founder and CEO of Golden OX LLC. But those titles didn't come easily. Behind every accomplishment is a story of grit, faith, and relentless love. My journey hasn't been polished or perfect—it's been hard-earned, shaped by battles most people never see. At the center of everything I do are my two sons, Antonio and Angel—both born with autism, both my greatest teachers and inspirations. Raising them has stretched me in ways I never imagined. It required a level of care, patience, and advocacy to redefine motherhood for me. Every day brings new challenges, new lessons, and new victories.

And yet, through it all, I've learned the true meaning of resilience. I've learned how to fight for my family's future while building a business from the ground up. I've learned that love can be the strongest motivator—and that sometimes, the things meant to break you end up building you instead. This chapter isn't just a story—it's a testimony. It's a window into my struggles, the strength I've discovered, and the legacy I'm creating. It's a tribute to my sons, my family, and every mother who's ever wondered if she's strong enough.

Spoiler: You are.

But strength alone wasn't enough. I needed solutions. I needed a path forward that honored my calling as a mother and my need to provide for my family. And that's how Golden OX LLC was born—out of necessity and ambition. As a mother of two boys with autism, I struggled to find a traditional job that offered the flexibility I needed to be there for them. It wasn't just about needing a "flexible schedule" but a job that could adapt to unpredictability. Therapy appointments, IEP meetings, medical emergencies, sensory meltdowns—these weren't things I could pencil in neatly between 9 and 5. They were my everyday reality.

And the hard part? The world isn't built for mothers like me. Employers often don't understand when you must cancel at the last minute due to a school call. They don't see the invisible labor it takes to coordinate therapies, advocate for services, and manage the emotional toll of caregiving. Every interview I attended felt like another door closing, not because I wasn't qualified, but because my life wasn't "convenient" enough for their systems.

I faced the impossible question so many special needs mothers face: How do I provide for my family while also being present for them? The systems that were supposed to support families like mine felt rigid, inaccessible, and unyielding. Yet, in those moments of rejection, I realized—I couldn't wait for someone else to create the space I needed. I had to build it myself.

Entrepreneurship wasn't just a career choice; it was a calling. It was survival. It was a rebellion against a system that made me feel like I had to choose between motherhood and a meaningful career. It was the only path that allowed me to honor my family and future. I knew that entrepreneurship was the best path to financial independence while also allowing me to prioritize my family. However, I needed the proper guidance to bring my vision to life.

That's when I found my business coach, Noelle Randall, who helped me turn my ideas into action. I was drawn to property management because of its long-term wealth-building potential and the opportunity to create a legacy for my children. For me, it wasn't just about owning properties but about owning possibilities. It was a shift in mindset from survival to strategy. From reacting to life to creating the life I wanted for my family.

I knew that property management wasn't a quick path to success. It required patience, grit, and vision. But that's exactly why it appealed to me. It mirrored the resilience I had been building in my personal life—showing up every day, even when it was hard, even when the results weren't immediate, even when I wasn't sure if it was working yet.

Entrepreneurship has taught me that resilience isn't just bouncing back—it's staying committed. It's holding the vision even when the circumstances don't match the dream. Property management became my classroom for resilience. Every challenge—whether it was learning new systems, navigating contracts, or dealing with setbacks—was another opportunity to grow stronger, more intelligent, and more determined.

I realized that building wealth wasn't just about money but also mindset. It was about believing I was worthy of abundance, even if I hadn't seen it modeled before. It was about trusting that every small step was building toward something greater, even if I couldn't see the whole picture yet.

Every time fear tried to creep in, every time doubt whispered that I couldn't do this, I reminded myself:

You've already overcome harder things.

You've already proven you don't quit.

This is just another step in the journey.

Property management wasn't just a business—it was a declaration. A declaration that I was stepping into ownership, leadership, and legacy. A declaration that my children would grow up watching their mother survive and thrive. Whenever things get tough, I remind myself of my "why." When the weight of responsibility feels overwhelming, the obstacles seem endless, and exhaustion whispers, "Maybe you're not cut out for this," I return to my reason. I think of Antonio and Angel. I think of the legacy I'm building for them. I think of the doors I'm opening so they'll never have to start at the bottom.

The struggles I've faced—both as a mother and a business owner—have taught me that giving up is never the answer. There have been moments when quitting felt easier; closing the laptop, turning off the phone, and walking away felt tempting. But then I'd look into my boys' eyes and remember: I'm not just doing this for me. I'm doing this so they'll know what's possible. I'm doing this so they'll see strength, perseverance, and faith in action.

My love for my family and my passion for my business is the fuel that keeps me going daily. Even on the hard days. Even when progress feels slow. Even when success feels far away, that combination of love and purpose turns struggle into strength, setbacks into lessons, and pressure into perseverance. When I remind myself of my "why," I realize I've already come too far to turn back. I also remember the importance of resilience.

When I gave birth to Angel, we almost didn't make it—both of our lives hung in the balance. I'll never forget lying in that hospital room, surrounded by machines and uncertainty, realizing just how fragile and precious life truly is. At that moment, I made a quiet promise: if we make it through this, I will fight for us every day.

But the fight didn't end there. After the trauma of childbirth, I struggled with my health. I had difficulty walking. Each step felt painful, slow, and uncertain. Doctors gave me timelines; some doubted how fully I'd recover. But I refused to let that be my story. I refused to be confined by what others predicted for me. I went to the gym. I worked hard. I pushed myself, day by day, inch by inch until I regained my strength. It wasn't just about healing my body—it was about proving to myself that I was stronger than the struggle.

Just when I thought we had overcome the biggest hurdle, life handed me another challenge. At three years old, Angel was diagnosed with autism. I sat in that doctor's office, listening to words I didn't yet fully understand, feeling both fear and fierce determination rising inside me. I knew at that moment that this was the next chapter in our journey where we would face it head-on.

Resilience isn't something I read in a book. It is something I have lived, breathed, and fought for. It is who I am. Every obstacle added another layer of strength. Every hardship taught me that giving up was never an option. That hospital bed, that gym, that diagnosis—they all became milestones marking my transformation. Each is a reminder: I have survived what was meant to break me. And because of that, I know I can handle whatever comes next.

I vividly remember the challenges I faced with Antonio. He struggled with speech delays and had to learn sign language to communicate. It took years of speech and other therapies before he could talk. I will never forget the moment I heard his voice for the first time—I had tears of joy streaming down my face.

There were days of exhaustion, frustration, and uncertainty, but I refuse to be defeated. I have found tools such as immersing myself in research, therapy sessions, and advocacy, with a determination to give my children the best opportunities possible. I have learned how to navigate the complexities of IEP meetings, therapy programs, and school systems while balancing the responsibilities of growing my business.

Golden OX LLC was not just a business—it was a lifeline. I knew I needed to build something sustainable for my future and that of my children. I envisioned a company that would allow me to break the cycle of struggle and create generational wealth.

I wanted Antonio and Angel to see that despite life's challenges, perseverance and hard work could lead to success. Every challenge I faced only strengthened my resolve. I reminded myself daily that setbacks were merely stepping stones to something greater. I sought mentors, read extensively, and took risks. There were financial struggles, moments of self-doubt, and times when the weight of responsibility felt overwhelming. But I refused to let fear dictate my path.

Beyond business and family, I've discovered a deeper calling—a calling to empower other women, especially mothers who are navigating a path similar to mine. I want to be more than just an example; I want to be a voice of encouragement. I want to be a reminder that even in the middle of the struggle, you are not alone. You don't have to give up on your dreams just because life throws you unexpected challenges.

When I first started this journey, I often felt isolated. It seemed like no one fully understood what it meant to juggle therapy appointments, school meetings, emotional ups and downs and still try to build a business from scratch. I didn't find many stories like mine being told. That loneliness could have swallowed me. But instead, it planted a seed: *What if I could be the voice I once needed to hear?*

I want other mothers to know that you don't have to wait until life calms down to start building something for yourself. You don't have to wait until every problem is solved, every crisis is over, and every challenge is behind you. You can build while you're in it. You can grow while you're healing. You can rise while you're still carrying the load.

I want them to know that success doesn't have to look like perfection. That messy progress is still progress. That small steps forward are still steps forward. That every effort they make—whether it's showing up for their kids, showing up for their business, or simply showing up for themselves—is worthy and valuable.

I also want them to know that their story matters. That their struggles are not a sign of failure but a testimony in the making. Their ability to persevere, to continue loving, and to build is a testament to their strength. This is why I share my story—not because it's easy to tell, but because I know it can light the way for someone else. If even one woman reads these words and feels hope rising in her heart, then every challenge I've faced has served a greater purpose.

We're all connected by the stories we tell and the stories we live. And if my journey can remind another mother that she, too, can carve out her path to success, then I've fulfilled a piece of my calling. Because at the end of the day, it's not just about building a business or creating wealth—it's about building a legacy of hope, strength, and possibility for the next woman, the next mother, the next generation.

These experiences have shaped my purpose and my determination. They are the reason I push forward, why I work hard every day, and why I refuse to give up. My journey has been marked by struggles, yet also by incredible triumphs. Through it all, I have learned that resilience, love, and unwavering commitment can overcome any obstacle. This is my motivation. This is my story. And this is just the beginning.

If I were to advise any entrepreneur, it would be this: celebrate the wins, big or small. Too often, we get caught up in the doing. We get so focused on serving others, meeting deadlines, hitting goals, and checking off lists that we forget to pause. We forget to honor the journey. We rush past our wins or downplay them, telling ourselves, "It's not enough yet." However, the truth is that every win is enough. Every win counts. And here's why it matters:

Celebrating wins isn't just a nice gesture—it's scientifically proven to fuel your success.

When we pause to celebrate, our brain releases dopamine—the "feel-good" chemical that boosts motivation, focus, and mood. It reinforces the idea that our hard work is paying off, and it encourages us to keep going. In a way, every celebration rewires our brain to associate effort with reward, making it more likely that we'll stay committed to our goals. I didn't realize it at first, but every time I acknowledged a win, no matter how small, it was like adding fuel to my fire. It shifted my mindset from one of scarcity to one of abundance. It reminded me that I was capable. It strengthened my belief that more wins were on the way.

Psychologists refer to this as the "progress principle"—the idea that we're happiest and most motivated when we see evidence of progress, not just at the finish line but throughout the entire journey. In business, this principle is powerful. Entrepreneurship isn't a straight road—it's filled with setbacks, pivots, and slow seasons. If we only celebrate significant milestones, we miss out on the momentum that small wins can provide.

Celebrating wins also creates emotional resilience. It helps balance out the inevitable hard days. When things don't go as planned, I can look back at my track record of wins and remind myself, "If I overcame before, I can do it again." It anchors me in possibility, even when the path forward feels unclear. Practically speaking, celebrating wins also improves business outcomes. It keeps morale high. It reduces burnout. It encourages creativity because it signals to your brain that success is possible. It builds confidence, and confidence is currency in business. So whether it's landing a new client, completing a project, surviving a tough week, or simply learning something new, take a moment to celebrate. Write it down. Speak it out loud. Share it with someone. Dance in your kitchen. Take yourself out for coffee. Take a moment to do something intentional to mark the occasion.

Every win is a seed for the next one. It tells your brain, your heart, and your spirit, "We're doing it." Even the smallest victory plants confidence where doubt once lived. It whispers, "See? We're growing. We're moving. We're building." These moments reinforce the truth that progress is happening—even if it's slower than you hoped or looks different than you imagined. And that belief? It will carry you further than any strategy or system ever could.

Because belief is what gets you out of bed on the hard days. Belief is what keeps you going. Belief is what keeps you going when no one's clapping yet. Belief is what drives you to try again after failure, show up after rejection, and continue building even when the results aren't immediate. Belief is the engine behind resilience. And as long as you believe, you'll always find a way forward.

That's the lesson I carry with me. That's the lesson I want every woman, every mother, and every dreamer reading this to hold onto: celebrate every win, no matter how small. Because those wins are proof, you're still standing, still fighting, still moving toward everything you were meant to become. I am still creating my path to success, going at the pace that allows me to live in a place of freedom.

Success is not a race—it's a journey, and you get to set the rhythm. You don't have to rush to meet anyone else's timeline. You don't have to shrink to fit someone else's mold. You are not confined to what society says your life should look like. You have the right to break free from expectations that tried to limit you. You can release the pressure to perform, to prove, to please.

You have the power to define success on your own terms, in your own time. You are allowed to feel at home in your own skin. You know what you've survived. You know what you've overcome.

So walk boldly, even when the road is unfamiliar. Stop waiting for permission or validation. Carve the path as you go, knowing that every step forward is a step of courage. Be proud of how far you've come. Be proud of the mountains you've climbed, the storms you've weathered, and the battles you've fought and won. Be proud of the person you're becoming.

This is your journey. This is your legacy in the making. And the best part? You are just getting started.

Now, I want to challenge you.

What's your "why"? What's the reason you keep going, even on the hardest days? Have you taken time to reconnect with it lately?

Where are you rushing past your wins instead of celebrating them? How might your journey change if you paused to honor every step forward, no matter how small?

What does success look like for you, not what others have told you it should be? Are you defining your path on your terms, or are you still confined by expectations that don't belong to you?

Where in your life are you underestimating your resilience? Can you look back at your story and see how strong, capable, and resourceful you've already been?

What legacy are you building right now—intentionally or unintentionally? How are your daily choices planting seeds for the next generation?

What's the next step you're willing to take? It's not the perfect step. Not the final step. Just the next one.

Because, like me, you don't have to have it all figured out to start building. You have to believe you're worthy of the journey.

So here's your invitation: Pause. Reflect. Celebrate. Then get up and keep going. Your story isn't over. You're just getting started.

Declaration:

I declare that I am powerful, resilient, and equipped for the journey ahead. I will no longer shrink to fit spaces that were never designed for me. I will walk boldly in my purpose, honoring every win along the way. I release the pressure to conform and embrace the freedom to create success on my terms. I am building a legacy of strength, hope, and possibility. Every step I take is a step forward. I am not behind—I am right on time. And the best is still yet to come.

HIT THE MARK

Your "why" is your anchor. When everything feels shaky, return to the reason you started.

Flexibility, not just ambition, is key to creating a life that aligns with both passion and purpose.

Progress isn't always loud or linear. Messy steps forward still move you forward.

You are allowed to define success in your terms, in your own time, and at your own pace.

Reflection

You've been carrying more than most people even realize, and you kept going. Celebrate your progress, and honor every moment you don't give up.

READY FOR MORE!

As you turn the final pages of Making It, take a deep breath. Let what you've just read settle in.

These weren't just stories—they were mirrors. Reflections of resilience that were born in the quiet moments when no one was watching. Of reinvention sparked not by perfect timing but by painful pivots. Of risks that didn't always come with a safety net. And of raw truth—the kind that doesn't always fit neatly into a social media caption.

Each Author dared to tell their whole truth about the journey—the unpolished, unfiltered process, not just the polished highlight reel. They opened the door to the backstage of their lives and let you witness what most people try to hide: the uncertainty, the second-guessing, the silent battles, and the strength it took to keep going anyway. They didn't just write for applause—they wrote for you. They wrote for the version of you that's been holding your breath, waiting for a sign that it's not too late to start again.

Some chapters were heavy, not because the writers lacked hope but because they chose to be honest about the weight they carried. Some hit too close to home, uncovering truths you've tried to avoid or wounds you've learned to work around. And some, perhaps, stirred up dormant dreams—the ones you buried beneath the rubble of bills, burnout, betrayal, or broken confidence.

But if those dreams still whisper to you after reading this book, then maybe—just maybe—they're not dead. They're just waiting for you to believe in them again.

Here's the good news: You're still making it.

Not "made it"—as if this is a one-time destination. No, making it is an ongoing choice to rise, rebuild, realign, and keep moving forward even when the path shifts or the plan fails. It's the decision to believe that your purpose is still valid, even if your path has taken some detours.

From Noelle's balancing act of business and motherhood to Justin's reminder that our beginnings don't limit our future, to Kymberly's journey of gratitude behind the wheel—each voice in this book has one common thread: they didn't quit. They redefined success on their terms.

So, now what? Take a moment to ask yourself:

What part of me was awakened while reading these pages?

What BS do I need to call out in my own life, like John did?

What cycle is it time to break, like Sherrie challenged?

What is the cost of staying stuck, as Tunita warned?

What gift is waiting for me, as Jennifer reminded us?

Don't let this book be a feel-good read you put back on the shelf. Let it be a mirror, a map, and a mandate.

A mirror to see yourself more clearly.

A map to chart what's next with more courage.

A mandate to take action—even if you have to plug your nose and jump.

Making it isn't a one-time win. It's a daily decision. And today, you get to decide again. What chapter will you write next? Even if you haven't put pen to paper, make no mistake—you're already writing your own Making It story. Every decision you've made, every detour you've taken, every lesson life has forced you to learn—that's all content. Real, lived, earned content. The kind you can't fake or fabricate. The kind that shapes legacy.

You may not have given it a title yet. You may not feel ready to share it publicly. But your story is unfolding, word by word, choice by choice, chapter by chapter.

So pause for a moment—not to perform, but to process.

Sit with the story of your life.

Reread the parts you try to skip over.

Highlight the wins you never celebrated.

Revisit the valleys where your character was refined.

Honor the fact that you're still here, still turning pages. You don't need anyone to validate your process. You don't need perfect grammar or a million followers to prove your story matters. All you need is the courage to own it—every beautiful, broken, becoming part of it. Healing begins when we stop editing out the complex parts of ourselves. And transformation begins the moment we stop telling ourselves we're too late, too messy, or too far gone to be made new. You are the Author of what comes next. This is your invitation—not just to reflect on what you've read but to rise from it. Let this book be the nudge you need to start living with more intention, more fire, and more faith.

Your story isn't over.

Noelle Randall

Noelle Randall is a successful real estate entrepreneur, a renowned Author, speaker, mentor, and influencer. Her journey from humble beginnings to building multiple thriving businesses has inspired thousands. With a mission to help others turn their dreams into reality, Noelle shares her expertise through books, videos, courses, and mentorship programs.

As the founder and CEO of NuuRez, Inc., Noelle has created one of the fastest-growing, crowd-funded real estate investment groups. Leveraging the same methods she teaches in her courses, NuuRez now manages a portfolio of luxury properties that generate consistent income through platforms like Airbnb and Vrbo.

A firm believer in accessible education, Noelle has built a massive YouTube following by sharing practical, actionable advice. Her free and paid resources—ranging from virtual events to comprehensive coaching programs—have helped countless aspiring entrepreneurs launch businesses, build rental fleets, and achieve financial freedom.

In addition to her work in real estate, Noelle is the founder of the Marley Simms Foundation, a nonprofit promoting children's literacy and author diversity. Most recently, she has expanded into the music industry by launching a record label to support emerging artists across various genres, providing them with the tools and exposure needed to thrive.

Noelle Randall is not just a businesswoman—she's a movement. Her impact spans multiple industries and communities, demonstrating that with the proper knowledge and determination, success is achievable for everyone.

Justin Mirche

Justin Mirche is a visionary entrepreneur, credit and funding expert, and the founder of Creative Credit Solutions and Justin Mirche Consulting. Raised in poverty and the first in his family to attend college, Justin's life is a powerful testament to grit, faith, and the relentless pursuit of purpose.

After walking away from a corporate career that didn't align with his values, Justin launched his first business with no outside investment—just conviction, discipline, and a calling to serve. Through his companies, he has helped countless individuals and business owners build solid financial foundations and access the credit and capital needed to scale with confidence.

Known for his Christ-centered leadership, relentless work ethic, and devotion to his family, Justin's mission is to inspire others to rewrite their stories, reclaim their power, and build lives filled with freedom, legacy, and peace. His message is simple but profound: your beginning does not dictate your end.

Dr. Sherrie Walton

Dr. Sherrie Walton is the visionary book-writing coach and powerhouse publisher behind this transformative anthology. As the founder of Walton Publishing House, she helps high-achieving entrepreneurs, executives, and culture-shifting leaders transform their stories and expertise into bestselling books, profitable brands, and unforgettable legacies.

With over two decades of corporate leadership experience, Dr. Sherrie is now a sought-after global business strategist, content architect, and culture curator. She is the creator of the *Grade Yourself*™ framework—an executive leadership and employee engagement system used to build self-aware, purpose-driven teams from the inside out.

Her work spans the U.S., the Caribbean, and international markets, equipping changemakers to license intellectual property, develop thought leadership platforms, and monetize their message with integrity and impact. Dr. Sherrie's voice has resonated with global audiences, and her work has been featured in prominent media and executive spaces for its unique blend of strategic clarity, transformational storytelling, and cultural relevance.

John Raymond

John is an esteemed executive with over 25 years of experience in management and leadership. His impressive track record spans across Fortune 500 companies and organizations recognized as Fortune's Best Places to Work. Armed with an MBA in finance from Washington State University, John has played a pivotal role in shaping business success through growth strategies, marketing expertise, and securing government contracts and grants.

In addition to his corporate prowess, John has excelled in acquiring and managing companies, with a notable involvement in real estate projects. His dedication extends beyond boardrooms, as he passionately engages in nonprofit work, fundraising, and fostering community growth. John's unwavering commitment to both business excellence and community upliftment has earned him a well-deserved reputation as an exceptional executive and trusted leader in the business landscape.

Tunita Bailey

Financial Strategist | Real Estate Expert | Empowerment Coach | Author

Tunita is widely known as The Money Lady—a powerhouse in the world of finance, real estate, and construction. With over two decades of experience turning everyday women into confident wealth builders, Tunita has become a trusted voice for those looking to transform ambition into action and financial pressure into freedom. As the CEO and founder of multiple successful ventures, including Capital City Mortgage and Capital City Construction, Tunita, is on a mission to help women build empires without sacrificing what matters most. She has guided thousands of entrepreneurs, homeowners, and professionals through the process of leveraging real estate, funding strategies, and smart investing to build lasting legacies.

Now, with her newest book, Marriage, Motherhood & Millions: The High Price of Having It All: Tunita Gets Personal. She pulls back the curtain on what it takes to balance ambition with love, business with motherhood, and power with peace. This raw, honest, and empowering guide is for every woman who's ever wondered if she could truly have it all—and what it might cost her to get there.

Whether she's speaking on stage, mentoring a new entrepreneur, or writing from her journey, Tunita delivers straight talk, fundamental strategies, and the kind of wisdom that only comes from living it. Her message is clear: you can build wealth, protect your peace, and live on your terms—without apology. Follow her journey, learn from her playbook.

Jennifer McPhail

Jennifer McPhail is a lifelong disability rights activist with over 32 years of experience as a community organizer with ADAPT, a national grassroots group fighting for the rights of people with disabilities. She is the founder and owner of McPhail Enterprises LLC, a company dedicated to creating wheelchair-accessible housing and promoting inclusive communities. Based in Austin, Texas, Jennifer brings her lived experience and professional expertise to her work as a speaker, trainer, and now first-time Author.

Kymberly Givens

Kymberly Givens is a professional truck driver and school bus driver who recently took a big leap and started her own trucking company. This is my first time writing a story, and I'm excited to share my journey of becoming my boss. I hope my journey inspires others to go after their dreams - even if it feels scary at first. Kymberly shares her inspiring journey of determination, hard work, and breaking barriers in a male-dominated industry.

When Kymberly isn't behind the wheel, she enjoys motivating others to chase their goals - no matter how big they are. Kymberly loves spending time with her family on road trips and vacations when she's not chasing her dreams.

Divonica Smith

Divonica Smith is an author, life coach, entrepreneur, and dynamic speaker known for transforming adversity into opportunity. A native of Omaha, Nebraska, Divonica overcame teenage pregnancy and a turbulent upbringing to establish a thriving Montessori-based childcare center and become a respected advocate for women's empowerment.

With a background in business management and public housing, Divonica brings both heart and strategy to everything she touches. She is also a certified DD service provider, dedicating her time to mentoring incarcerated women and young mothers, helping them develop life skills, confidence, and purpose.

Through her nonprofit work, entrepreneurial leadership, and motivational speaking, Divonica empowers others to rise above their circumstances and build lives they're proud of. Her journey is living proof that faith, determination, and vision can rewrite any story.

Alinda Rowley-Jensen

Alinda Rowley-Jensen is the CEO and founder of ARJ Investing. This multimillion-dollar real estate company has transformed the Utah housing market through innovative solutions and heart-centered leadership. Known for her strategic expertise and compassionate approach, Alinda has helped hundreds of families avoid foreclosure and regain financial stability, turning hardship into hope.

Through ARJ Investing, Alinda has pioneered a unique model that enables investors to acquire existing mortgages, creating mutually beneficial opportunities for both homeowners and investors. Her business is rooted in integrity, impact, and a deep commitment to the community, making her a trusted name in real estate across the state.

Driven by resilience and a bold entrepreneurial spirit, Alinda is passionate about empowering women, preserving homeownership, and building lasting wealth through real estate. Her journey from the ground up is a powerful reminder that with vision, strategy, and heart, anything is possible.

Mercedes Sanchez

Mercedes is a determined entrepreneur and devoted mother of two young boys with autism. Juggling the responsibilities of caregiving and business, she made the bold decision to relocate to California, driven by a desire to pursue her professional goals more intentionally. Each day, she faces the unique challenges of raising children with special needs, yet her resilience never wavers.

For Mercedes, life isn't easy—but giving up isn't an option. She sees it as a boxing match inspired by the legendary Muhammad Ali. Just like in the ring, life demands strategy, strength, and heart. "To be champions," she often reminds herself, "we have to keep fighting." That mindset fuels her journey—a journey defined by growth, sacrifice, and a deep commitment to building a better future for her family.

With unwavering love for her children and a fire in her spirit, Mercedes continues to rise each day, facing every round life throws her way with courage and purpose.

Your Story Could Be Next!

You've just read powerful stories of resilience, reinvention, and rising against the odds. Now it's your turn.

If you have a story inside you—a journey of struggle, strength, success, or self-discovery—this is your invitation to be part of **Noelle Randall's next book anthology**. We're looking for bold voices, authentic experiences, and people ready to inspire the world through their truth.

Share your story. Amplify your voice. Make your mark.

Apply now to join the movement.

NoellesBookSeries.com

www.ingramcontent.com/pod-product-compliance
Lightning Source LLC
Chambersburg PA
CBHW070952180426
43194CB00042B/2275